THE WINDOW
OF CHILDHOOD

THE WINDOW OF CHILDHOOD

GLIMPSES OF WONDER AND COURAGE

Olson Huff, M.D.

Westminster/John Knox Press
Louisville, Kentucky

Acknowledgment is made to the American Medical Association for the use of material in the preface, first published in *The Journal of the American Medical Association,* vol. 251 (March 16, 1984), p. 1423. Copyright 1984, American Medical Association.

Book design by Gene Harris

First edition

Published by Westminster/John Knox Press
Louisville, Kentucky

PRINTED IN THE UNITED STATES OF AMERICA

9 8 7 6 5 4 3 2 1

Library of Congress Cataloging-in-Publication Data

Huff, Olson, 1936–
   The window of childhood : glimpses of wonder and courage / Olson Huff. — 1st ed.
        p.   cm.
   ISBN 0-664-25094-7

   1. Children—United States.   I. Title.
HQ792.U5H84 1990
305.23′0973—dc20   89-25075
                                                          CIP

To

Marylyn

Whose gentle insistence—"Do it, do it"—
has borne fruit

And to

David, Stephen, and Daniel

Who taught me that being a pediatrician
did not make me a better father,
but that being a father has helped me
to be a better pediatrician

Contents

Preface

Occasionally, when my day seems such a jumble of incessantly crying children, demanding problems, and lengthening hours as to make me wonder about my choice of profession, I remember the face of a certain child and I am renewed.

My career was to be in medicine; I knew that and had thought of nothing else since long before I entered the university. Pediatrics was only a blur of an idea, however, during college, when one day my extracurricular activities took me to a local children's hospital.

I don't recall his name. He sat rigidly with his wheelchair backed up against the wall, white enameled steel beds surrounding him like bars of a prison. He cared little for the movies I brought from the university film library and held back from the banter and rowdy play of the other children, even of those in wheelchairs like his own. His dark eyes burned when I dared to look at him, and I knew he needed more from me than movies. I pretended not to notice him, finding the other side of the room more comfortable.

Then the man came. A member of a local service group, it was his turn to go with me to the hospital. Kind and easy, he seemed not to fear the fire in the boy's eyes, and they instantly became close. Perhaps the father in him enabled him to show his care for the boy where my youth was a block. No matter. They laughed, the wheelchair rolled, and the boy's eyes, though still bright, softened.

On the next visit I found the boy in his chair in the middle of the room, looking past me eagerly to find the face of my companion, who had a mysterious something, a medicine not yet bottled, that pushed away the fear and the loneliness. Again, there was laughter and a gift: a watch for the boy to wear around his bony wrist like a talisman to show as he did battle with the demons of contortion that afflicted his scarecrow frame.

The man did not come again. I had seen it in his eyes as he left that night; I knew he had gotten too close for comfort, and I wondered what secrets were too burdensome to risk exposing to the piercing gaze of the boy. Later he called, to give an excuse and to say, "Tell the boy hello." That was all. I was left to face those eyes alone, eyes that searched for the face beyond mine; alone to mumble a reply to the nearly hysterical cry, "Where is he?" And alone to watch the wheelchair retreat to the wall, surrounded by white enameled bars.

That was years ago, and I don't recall the boy's name. But like a flicker of blue sky pushing through gray clouds, my mind is occasionally stimulated by the memory of his searching eyes, and I am challenged anew—challenged to be the man whose presence can release some of the fear and hurt in the children who see me daily, challenged to reassure them that they no longer need to search beyond my face to find one who is a friend.

Introduction

I had not intended to stop by the newborn nursery, for my visit to the hospital was meant for a friend in need of a few cheerful words. Habit drew me there anyway, and I arrived right at feeding time. Only a few days remained before Christmas. The hallways and windows were colorfully and cleverly decorated, featuring babies as the central theme of the holiday season. Sunshine sparkled through the skylight and pushed away the shadows from the face of one newly arrived infant, sheltered in its bassinet parked in the hallway, waiting for the trip to its mom's room. Lounging against the wall, within easy hovering distance, was a young man. As I stopped to admire the baby, he spoke.

"Prettiest baby I ever saw. She's already smiled at me and she isn't even six hours old yet! She's going to be just as smart as her brother. He's three, you know. Oh, I'm a lucky man for sure, a lucky man."

He turned to follow the aide and his baby, and I went the other direction to finish my visit, thinking about his words and especially about children.

This baby had evoked deep and previously unimaginable emotions in her father. With only a questionable attempt to smile, she could command the attention of all around her. With a simple cry, she could send everyone scurrying to meet her needs. Still, she and her countless comrades are viewed as helpless and totally dependent. Rarely, I thought, are children understood, even by those of us who think we know them well. Their gifts are misinterpreted, their words unheard, and their actions often viewed as bothersome or insignificant. Sadly, such thinking robs adults of the very traits they claim but never seem to hold—the strength and power of their own singular created selves. Instead of being helpless, children, even newborn babies, have a marvelous power to influence their world. As we look carefully at the strength of children, we are invited to claim our own unique strength.

Childhood is often viewed as a stage to be gotten through, and children like green tomatoes on a vine waiting to mature. Instead, I see childhood as a time of life which has its own identity. It is a time to put down deep and permanent roots and a time to develop the God-given shape of who we really are. As we experience children, as we see them not as small creatures but as vibrant and dynamic persons, we can experience our own roots and begin to discover ourselves. Children tell us of life. They tell us of love, joy, pain, death, hope, friendship, and the discovery of new things. As we listen to the children in our lives, we may find the courage to face the hopes and fears that are often locked deep within us.

That is why I have written this book: to provide a window to childhood through which we may look to appreciate children and enrich ourselves. In it you will meet children and families who are my friends and will learn something of how their strength and courage define my life, just as I hope they will add dimension to yours. Their stories are the events and experiences of many, their characters blended from the truth that makes childhood so unique. The individuals who have contributed to that blend have brought much joy to my life, and to each of them I say thanks.

Meet them now. Hear their words and listen carefully to what they have to say. Above all, join in their games and share in their imaginations, for that may allow you to hear the child of your own beginnings and thereby renew a long-forgotten friendship.

1

"And It Was Good"

"And God saw everything that he had made, and behold, it was very good."

Genesis 1:31

Water, soap, scrub. Again. And for good measure, one more time. Water dripped from my elbows as I donned a freshly laundered gown. Holding up my thoroughly scrubbed hands to protect them from touching the doorway, I stepped into the nursery.

Morning sunshine was scattered cheerfully on numerous cribs, but their occupants paid little attention. Some slept quietly, sighing occasionally, dreaming, I suppose, of things too secret to remember. Others screeched loud protest at anyone in earshot, and a few cast rapid glances through half-closed eyelids, hoping to be first in line for feeding time. My business was with one wide awake but quiet little fellow, three days old and scheduled for discharge, who lay nestled comfortably in his clean white blankets.

"She's lucky, that mom." The comment came from the nurse's aide.

"Why do you say so?" I asked.

"Nuzzles you right in the soft of the neck," she said. "Burps, looks around awhile, and goes back to sleep. No hysterics or screaming fits for him. He's a soft, gentle little one, with a backbone made of steel."

You mark my word, doctor, he'll take care of himself."

With her sage observations in mind, I watched baby Alan for a few moments, relaxing in his substitute womb. He did seem to have a certain style or presence about him. I had an impression of, if not exactly independence, at least of plenty of self-reliance. I understood what the nurse's aide was saying. This baby was destined to exert quite an effect on his parents.

And that is what we proceeded to find out.

He ignored the smiles and comments about his appearance offered by the bustling staff of the postpartum floor as we made our way to his mother's room. Resting in the crook of my arm, he seemed quite content despite the movement, and he made no objection as I drew him a bit closer to my body to avoid his bumping into anyone.

Alan's parents were not strangers. I had met them in a prenatal interview in my office when together we had discussed their expectations about the birth of their child. Now they were waiting eagerly, and I suspected a bit anxiously, to begin their long-awaited task.

"Good morning" was hardly spoken before Alan's mom reached for her son. Any awkwardness she felt was mostly concealed by her excitement. Her movement attracted Alan's attention. He stared directly into his mother's eyes and she returned the look. It was over quickly, that glance, but it lasted long enough for me to see the flush of satisfaction and pure delight that came to her face. Alan had ignited a powerful spark that allowed her to begin to know him. Unlike the physical bond of the last nine months, this new dimension of their relationship opened the potential for the nurturing she wanted to give.

"He doesn't seem to be as helpless as I thought." She faltered a moment, then continued. "I get the distinct feeling that he knows who I am and is at least a little confident that I'll take good care of him. Did you see the way he looked at me?"

I nodded to her in affirmation.

There is something very real about the bonding of human families. In the new infant rests a power greater than that which can be explained by the instinct of parents to protect and provide. It differs from the squawking furor of a mother hen with chicks sheltered beneath her wings. It is not the same as the patterning that aligns goslings in single file, waddling after their hurrying protector. At the earliest beginning of breathing life, there exists in human form the opportunity for parents and babies to know a secret part of each other. It is a mysterious secret, one that forges alliances for acceptance and mutual sharing while simultaneously encouraging movement toward independence and loneliness. Newborn babies possess it as a gift; grownups are privileged to have it awakened by the look in their own child's eyes.

I remember when that first became apparent in our family. David, our firstborn child, strapped securely into the back seat of our little blue VW bug, was making one of his first shopping trips with us. As we neared the Air Force base where I was stationed, my wife turned to me, a peculiar look on her face and fire in her shining eyes.

"I never understood it before," she said, "but now I know! Before David was born, I could not understand how it would be possible for me to harm anyone, even to protect myself. For him, however, I'd fight any battle, to the limits of my strength, to keep him safe."

A mysterious secret. Not an accident of birth or an instinct of nature, but a life-giving force. Helpless babies? Rather the opposite, I think.

Alan curled his tiny fingers around the large ones of his father. The young man was pleased and touched. He held Alan, shyly, not exactly sure how to respond. Alan solved the problem nicely, however, by noisily filling his diaper. The ice was broken for all three of them as once again their son had proven, knowingly or not, his ability to make his presence known.

We talked further, about routine matters.

"Does he have to burp after every ounce of formula?"

"There's a party at Jane's house Sunday. May we take him?"

"What about a suntan?" This question from Dad. "He'd look great with a suntan!"

"Do I have to keep his head covered when he goes outside?"

"What about cereal?"

There are a lot of questions to be answered before the road to growing up can be completely paved.

Finally, I reached for Alan to return him to the nursery, write his discharge, and finish my morning rounds.

"So you both agree, then, that he is not as helpless as he first appeared?"

They smiled in response. As with most of us, the idea that this power could be present in a newborn baby had been nonexistent. They now knew differently, a fact that augured well for the future.

Alan had been the one who looked at them. They had responded. With no words, no ability to move from his crib, not even the knowledge of the hours of his nights and days, Alan had evoked their behavior and channeled their response. With his cries, he now would guide their hours and define their days. With his maturing hand movements he would grasp more than objects as he maneuvered them into acknowledging and meeting his needs. The ability to roll to and fro and to position his head upright would strengthen his hold on them. I could envision their responses when he learned to sit, to crawl, and then to walk, and I could anticipate their excitement at his accomplishments and their apprehension of his headlong rush toward self-maintenance.

No small wonder, this newly born child, I thought. Like his neighbors in the nursery, he is a veritable powerhouse of stored energy, ready to be unleashed, waiting to get on with it.

Alan and I walked back toward the nursery.

"Well done, my young friend," I whispered to him. "I'm always happy to show others that your kind of folk are not blank sheets of paper on which to write whatever fantasy is most in vogue. I know you have many abilities and I know how clearly you can voice your aims and intentions. You're born wanting to grow up, to exercise your God-given personality, to fashion your own niche in the world. I suspect you have something to say about your own growing up and aren't going to think kindly of those who try to misdirect you. Fair enough. But don't push it too hard. Your parents are good people and they will learn quickly, but give them some time to strike a balance between their ideas and your needs."

Alan yawned and slept.

"Did you say something, doctor?" The nurse, not sure what else to ask, waited for my reply.

"Did I say something? I hope so. I surely hope so. Do you think," I asked her suddenly, stopping at the nursery door as the new thought came to me, "that parents like Alan's, who talk to their babies and call them by name, are less frightened when they go home than those who don't?"

"Yes, I think so," she answered. "In calling their baby by name, they are able to see a person. And it's harder to be afraid of people we know."

"Yes," I replied, "and it keeps on happening. They don't get as buffeted by the fevers, the falls, the bleeding noses and croupy coughs that inhabit the dismal swamps of childhood. And they aren't as likely to be undone by the nightmares, unseen monsters, and bed-wetting that so often accompany their youngster's transition from the world of magic to grown-up reality. The strength or ability or whatever you want to call it to be separate that parents sense in their baby just allows parents to use their own strength to act. So it's like a co-op. Babies aren't helpless, and as Mom and Dad respond to that knowledge, neither are they.

"Alan," I said, "you are a lucky soul. Your parents are strong and your nurse is wise. And your doctor is getting further behind by the minute!"

He did not awaken as I placed him back in his crib. The nurse's aide was right. Gentleness and softness, and a hard core of strength; she had read him well.

On the desk in my office is a small plaque given to me by the mother of one of my patients. It reads, *I know I'm somebody, 'cause God don't make no junk!*

I suspected strongly that Alan would have no cause to argue with that sentiment, now or in the future.

2

Fear

I do not know which hour of the night is darkest. Inside the hospital, with the unblinking incandescent light flooding each corner of the newborn intensive care nursery, time is measured more by the weariness of the body and the degree of the patients' need than by the hands of the clock or the light of day. When Annie Lea was born, it was like that. I remember also that the streets were awash with streaking spring rains as I hurried to catch up with her birth.

Too early. Tiny, limp, hardly breathing, she gasped for each lungful of oxygen we poured into the plastic bubble around her head. With the intensity of wanting this child to live, I slipped a tiny plastic tube into an even smaller artery. Precious drops of blood out for testing, sustaining and balancing fluids in, the newly installed lifeline held her to us. She, in that strange plastic box with large eye ports, and we, with our mixture of medicines and testings, clung to each other with every fiber of our beings. Crises came and went. Infection threatened, her lungs became congested and refused to accept all the oxygen she needed, and her cry at times weakened to the point of inaudibility. Still, she held onto the lifeline. Hours became days and days pushed toward being a week as, slowly, pink began to replace the blue-gray of her fingernails and she began to win.

Close to her but still on the periphery, with a question here and a smile there, were her parents. Slowly they became more central to Annie's care as the nursery staff and I retreated to the concerns of others. A party of sorts marked the day that Annie moved through the doorway of the intensive care nursery and began her trip to the crib where she now belonged. If I noticed the tight, frightened smile on her mother's face, I simply registered it as new-mother jitters, nothing more.

Days and weeks and telephone calls passed. Annie continued to grow, had only a tiny bit of colic, and seemed to smile earlier than most. She delighted the nurses in the office with her eager reach, and kept her mother busy feeding and bathing her and picking up the musical toys she loved to drop from the tray of her high chair. Too busy, perhaps, because I still failed to reach beneath the apparent steadiness to wonder why there were so many phone calls, so many questions.

"What exactly should the temperature of the milk and the air in the room be? Precisely how many hours of sleep does she need? How long should I wash hands before touching her? How do I—politely, of course—keep others at a distance?"

Ordinary questions, touched with a hint of unsureness. I did not inquire, I only answered.

"Doc, we have to see you right away!" It was Annie's father calling, after midnight, panic rising in his voice.

Imagining the worst, I agreed to see them at once, in the emergency room just five minutes from my home.

Of the four of us, Annie Lea was clearly in the best shape. I, disgruntled, could diagnose only a mild cold and suggest simple remedies. Dad seemed willing enough to try them and appeared both chagrined and relieved. Not so with Annie's mother. Finally, things began to fall into place as in her terror-stricken eyes I saw all the questions I had answered and all those she had been too frightened to ask. Annie only needed some steam vapor and extra fluid, but her mother

needed understanding and recognition of the overwhelming fear that turned even the simplest of illnesses into life-threatening catastrophe. At last I
could take a hint.

In succeeding days and on separate visits, I listened
to what Annie Lea's mother had to say.

"I didn't think she would live." Eyes rimmed with
tears, she twisted a tissue in her hands, trying not to
lose control. "We prayed so hard, and still I was so
scared. John seemed to accept things day by day, but
each time I saw her, it was like a part of me was struggling with her to breathe. When she began to improve, and you and the nurses seemed less concerned
about her, I started to hope for the first time.

"But then when we finally took her home I was convinced she couldn't make it without all those tubes
and lights and buzzers. At first, I tried to sit by her
crib, especially at night, to make sure she wouldn't
stop breathing or spit up and choke. I felt foolish
about it, but I couldn't help myself. John tried to
cheer me up, to humor me, but I think he was scared
for her too and just didn't know how to show it. I tried
to ask questions but I didn't know how. Here in the
office, everything seemed just fine, but at night I'd
hear her cough or sneeze and I just knew she would
die!"

I handed her the box of tissues. She sat quietly,
tracing her thoughts, remembering the times before
Annie's birth.

"The pregnancy never felt right," she continued.
"Everyone kept trying to reassure me, but there was
something indefinable that didn't fit. It's an awesome
thing to grow a person right inside your body, and I
know I felt some sense of struggle or uneasiness that
seemed to say that Annie needed help. Neither I nor
anyone else knew what to do, of course. When labor
started early, I wasn't surprised, just frightened for
her."

I wondered. Could it possibly be that some commu-

nication between Annie and her mother had occurred? Could it be that the distress that resulted in
the premature birth had been, ever so vaguely, felt by
Annie's mother? Is there some instinctive awareness
during the process of pregnancy that weds mother
and child more than we can know or understand? I do
not know. If it exists, it would be impossible to quan-
tify. What I was witnessing, however, was an understanding on the part of a mother that her child had
been in danger and that she had to continue in the
role of guardian and protector. For the present, that
role had become overwhelming. Fear had made her
doubt her ability to respond. Now she clearly needed
time to talk, to have her questions respected, and to
have her fears addressed. A beginning-point in the
process that would produce healthy growth for Annie
and her mother had been established.

I thought of the plastic line that had brought our
technology to this small baby. In high-risk infants like
Annie Lea, parents are shut out by our feverish attempts to save their baby's life, try as we might to include them. It is easy for them to become dependent
upon medical skill and technology and to doubt their
ability to know their child and to act appropriately.
Alone at home, they feel inadequate and afraid.

Fear can instruct us or it can consume us. It can
move us to action or paralyze us. When her fear was
acknowledged, Annie Lea's mother was once again
able to trust her own knowledge of her child. That vi-
tal connection, a more powerful and nontechnical
connector that would hold the real structure of life,
was reestablished. Annie's mother relaxed visibly,
signaling the end of our conversation. Whatever the
next crisis, she felt more confident to exercise her
own judgment as to how to handle it. That was a significant step for her, and one that would pay dividends in the future, because Annie would inevitably
develop more independence and seek more control
over her own life.

I do not know, then, when light is the least and the night is most dark. I do know, however, that fear feels like the darkest part of the night, as it squeezes panic into the corners of people's lives, especially when they are the most vulnerable. Annie's birth in the spring of the year was an event beset with danger, one that could have forced out the brightness she was intended to bring. Fortunately, that did not happen. Her growing encouraged the release of fear, and the light I subsequently observed in her mother's eyes made me listen more carefully to others' questions, to hear what they were truly saying.

3

Why?

"Stick, Mommy! Stick! Stick!"

She ran, but she reached the playhouse too late, in time only to see her retarded son's uncomprehending and painful withdrawal from the pretty "stick" he tried to hold. Conquering her intense fear, she grabbed him up and fled in one direction, the snake disappearing in another.

His hand and forearm were swollen and discolored by the time I reached the emergency room. Blood was drawn, IV fluids started, and antivenin administered. Through it all, Chuck, who was pretty well accustomed to us and our many attempts to help him, tried to smile, babbling all the while in his usual way. The snake was a copperhead, and although Chuck would be ill and would need specific medical care, he was not likely to face a critical threat from his encounter. I wasn't so sure, however, about Chuck's mom.

She sat rigidly, color drained from her face, waiting.

"It's not as bad as it could be, Margaret. He'll do just fine."

She nodded. No sign of relief, no tears, no relaxing. Just nodding her head.

"You OK now?" I asked.

She glanced at me briefly. The pain in her eyes was her only answer.

"Let's go get him settled," I suggested, and led the

way to the children's ward. She knew the way well, for here she practically had a permanent room, a place where Chuck often struggled to survive, and she to discover why.

Chuck's mischievous smile and impulsive spirit belied the significance of his need, and often buoyed our confidence that he would improve. Today, however, that expectation seemed less substantial. Judging from the weariness that seemed to have settled to the core of her being, Chuck's mother was feeling the same way. Always, she had accepted his mental delay, had confronted each new seizure with steady faith in our ability to stop it, and had dealt firmly with his erratic and petulant temper. She had maintained an unassailable hope that her son would gain in self-reliance and that his judgment would sharpen enough to give him the skills necessary to make his way in a busy and confusing world. It had been that hope from which she had drawn the courage and the strength to face Chuck's many difficulties. Today, the supply seemed exhausted.

She sat by Chuck's bed, watching the slow drip of the IV, noting his muttering and jumping in sleep. She was no longer rigid, just tired and hurt.

"You going home?"

She shook her head. "No," she said, "Chuck gets too scared if he wakes up and I'm not here."

True. Chuck did not understand that a pretty "stick" could hurt, and he was not aware that any place other than his home was friendly. He was disturbed by the movements, lights, and noises at the hospital, and he did not comprehend the need to have his arm tied to his bed for the IV fluids. He would be afraid, and he would need her caring smile and the soft music of her voice.

There were no known reasons why Chuck was retarded. His birth had followed a normal and much desired pregnancy, and the early months of his life gave no hint of mental delay. When he was a year old, he had his first seizure, and soon thereafter, another. He began to talk later than normal and seemed preoccupied with his own thoughts, ignoring his older sister and clinging frantically to his mother when anything unusual occurred. Tests, exhaustive and thorough, revealed only a "seizure focus," and no reason why.

The older Chuck became, the more difficult the seizures were to control, and his hospital stays became longer and more frequent. In spite of that, Chuck did acquire some new knowledge and, under his mother's persistent and patient approach, developed a friendly, responsive personality. However, he was never comfortable being far from her when trouble seemed near.

We had often talked about Chuck and why he should be so afflicted. There are, of course, known causes of developmental delays. Some children, such as those with Down's syndrome, have a structural difference in the arrangement of their chromosomes. Other youngsters have metabolic disorders or malformations in the growth of the brain and nervous system. Still others may have infections such as meningitis or encephalitis that impair brain function. Certainly accidents and other injuries add to the list of known causes. But after all these are taken into consideration, the scales still tip toward those who ask, again and again, Why?

Within the framework of that question lies an even more fundamental one. What did I do to cause this? Inevitably, the question of guilt and the fear of finding its answer mingle to keep the anguish of grief from moving to the acceptance and tolerance that can give healing to hurting families. That anguish finally forms a dead, dull ache that will hear no words of reassurance and accept no gifts of pardon.

So I decided to be late for dinner. "Are you giving up?" I asked.

"What do you mean?" Some life flickered in the dull eyes.

"Just that. You think it's your fault that Chuck got bitten by the copperhead. Deep inside, you're afraid it's your fault that he is retarded. God, you think, is punishing you for some awful childhood wrong that you can't even remember, and so you are giving up. Oh, not on Chuck. On yourself. Your dreams, your hopes—they don't matter any more. You think your daughter doesn't need you much any more, and your husband has his work. So who does need you, since you're to blame for it all, right?"

I paused.

"Did I ever say that?" she whispered.

"Not directly," I said, kinder now. "But you think it a lot." I shifted in my chair, observing the nurse who had come to check the IV. "You love Chuck and feel so responsible for him and so awfully mad at God that things got mixed up in your plans for life. All of us cope with that kind of confusion and loss by reacting in a variety of ways and with a mixture of feelings. Anger is appropriate, but we forget that God can accept our anger, so we feel very guilty for having such feelings and find ourselves wanting to be punished in a misguided attempt to be justified in our own guilt. Finally we reach a point where things are so muddled we just plain don't care any more. That's a kind of depression, I suppose, but in reality I think we just give up."

She nodded, not woodenly but with a growing sense of comprehension.

"You know," I continued, "I don't know why Chuck has a problem. I rack my brain and pick the brains of others to find out what's wrong. In so doing, I become more and more aware of the awesomeness of the way our bodies function, most of all the mind. As I grapple with that knowledge, I am aware of how little I can make it change. Sure, I give medicines that alter some functions and even sometimes control Chuck's seizures. But I cannot make the cells new, or make their intimate, intricate details change, and that is what I really wanted to tell you. You can blame yourself all you want, but to no avail. You see, you don't have the power to have structured his cells or to have organized the fantastic pattern of his marvelous character, and you certainly don't have the power to have made him different in any way. Your power lies in the fact that you care. That is the power Chuck has allowed to grow in you. Use it, not in fear, but in hope. OK?"

She was tired and vulnerable and I had risked having her not hear me. I waited. I caught just a hint of mist in her eyes as she smiled at me. Chuck, sleeping peacefully now, instinctively reached his free hand to her, and she held it. I went home to eat. Somehow, a late meal didn't seem like such a bad idea after all.

4

Listen to the Children

The narrow little town stretched along Main Street, its courthouse serving as the center of attention and concern for its citizens. On one side rose a wall of mountains; the other side was anchored by the railroad, which ran between the highway and a swift river that raced past jagged cliffs on the other side. Guided by river and railroad, the highway bent sharply, wound through a ravine, and suddenly deposited the unwary traveler onto Main Street near the courthouse. The town was quickly left behind if one had no business there. Such was not the case for me on a day late in winter, for the courthouse, with its blindfolded lady and her scales, was my destination. Places to park were at a premium, and the gathering of people on the sidewalk spoke of the interest and fear surrounding the event that required my presence. Patches of snow, melting rapidly in the warm sunshine, sent rivulets of water along the gutter. Tired-looking people dropped shoulders to allow me clear passage. One man, cigarette drooping from his mouth and one eye partially closed to keep out the smoke, said in response to my query that the courtroom was at the top of the stairs to the right.

I was there because of Emily and Audrey and Jack and Emory. They were not actually my patients, but their plight was the same as that of many who were or someday would be.

Their parents were poor. They had been abused.
Sexually molested. Their frail dignity assaulted and
their smiles erased. Frightened, they had kept quiet.
But their bodies gave away the secret. They had
nightmares and screamed and soiled their pants and
wet their beds and finally, in whispers, shared their
shame.

But they were not believed.

"Welfare folks, you know, Doc. Besides, they're
just young'uns, and you know they don't tell the
truth."

Right.

From the moment I had left home that day, time re-
versed itself. Snatches of my own childhood, stirred
to life by the hovering mountains and stray sunbeams
pushing through tall pine trees, danced into my mind.
The roar of powerful steam-driven locomotives, their
tops belching smoke and their whistles screaming defiance to the wind, filled my memory, as the road par-
alleled graceful curves of steel. River, wind, sun, and
railroad combined to form a tapestry that defined my
beginnings and gave purpose to the course I now followed. I was here in this town to say something about
children. To say no, they don't lie (unless forced to do
so) and no, being poor doesn't make them less worthy
of protection or care. Part of my childhood, the part
that said being poor shouldn't have to mean being
afraid, came with me.

The case in question was not as important as the
very fact that such an event was even necessary. The
children had been sexually assaulted. The profession-
als had no doubt of this—the pediatricians, social
workers, and teachers who had examined their bodies
and heard their stories. Yet the townfolk did not believe them. It was too much for the people on the narrow single street and the surrounding hills to accept.
Such a happening could not be. Not here, not in this
place. Possibly in the big cities, but not here. Here
each family and its history were known to all, and

such things could not exist, or the pain of disclosu. would shatter the facade of decency. Deny it, stifle the fear it suggests, slam shut any door of reasoning that might force light into corners where darkness dwells.

They were asked to swear, Emily, Audrey, Jack, and Emory, one hand on the Bible, the other toward heaven. Too young to read, bodies trembling, they were exhibited for all to see, questioned by lawyers fighting with them over whatever scrap of intelligible speech they could utter through lips almost too frozen by fear to move.

"Now Emory, you're a good boy, aren't you? You don't tell stories and you always mind your mama, don't you?"

The insidious questions touched Emory in the center of his five-year-old's desire to please. Not trusting his trembling lips, he nodded affirmation.

"What did you say?"

The courtroom shook with the thunder of the question.

"Can't hear you, son. Do you tell stories? Yes or no?"

"Y-Y-yes, I—I mean no," stammered Emory, tears welling in his eyes.

"Didn't you tell stories about my friend over here?" The accused was indicated.

"Objection!"

"Overruled."

"Well, answer me, Emory; you told stories, didn't you?"

Emory froze. Slowly, a visible circle of darkness spread across the front of his pants. He could not speak. His body shook, and he was more afraid than he had been when the man had touched him and done strange things to him.

"Your honor, I move for dismissal. These children are just making up stories."

"Denied. Court is recessed for ten minutes."

Audrey was next and she fared no better.

"Now, tell us, Audrey, where my friend touched you and what he did and what you did. Or maybe you could just show us."

Too young to understand the reason but old enough to know shame, Audrey simply screamed. Again and again.

Once more, court was recessed.

In the end, they said anything, responded to questions with whatever answer they thought would please, just to be free—free of the overwhelming, staring mass of strangers who filled to overflowing the ancient, dreary room, free of anything that reminded them of the awful reasons they were here. Whatever they said did not matter. They were not believed.

Like the roads of that town, we too are narrow and blind. The system that is supposed to protect and aid becomes the aggressor, abusing the souls of these children as much as the accused has abused their bodies. We are blind because we cannot hear their feeble words trying to say how much it hurts, blind because we do not see and know their anxious vulnerability. We do not worry that they may be harmed. After all, they are young; they will outgrow it.

Right.

Who are the abused? Are there really very many? Are there really any consequences of their hurt? The answers to these questions are around us wherever we go. One of every four girls and one of every seven boys is sexually abused during childhood. They are victims of frustration, of sick minds, of trapped and frozen ambition. They are scarred, and many cross from lives of potential self-respect to lives that remain in the shadows. Their destiny is the sadness of prostitution, the neurosis of lack of trust. Many eventually become abusers themselves.

It is an epidemic, this problem of child abuse, an epidemic in desperate need of a cure. The courtroom hardly seems the place to provide the justice and the treatment for which both victim and abuser cry out:

justice that restores and justice that corrects. Tearing away the barriers of fear and hysteria that cloud reason and deny justice seems impossible in the charged atmosphere and defensive climate in front of the judge's bench. Especially remote seems the kind of justice that sits blindfolded atop the gleaming dome of the courthouse in the little mountain town whose street and river and railroad are the ribbons that hold back the towering walls of stone.

My car climbed the highway swiftly as I watched the receding image of the town in the rearview mirror. The people there were too close, too suspicious of one another's motives, too conditioned by the narrowness of their lives to believe that children could be "bothered like that." Memories from my childhood, fostered in mountain towns like these, made me soften toward those people as I drove.

I tried to understand. Despite any understanding or acceptance, however, hard reality that could not hide behind the hills of ignorance remained. As surely as I had done, those children too would travel to a point in their lives where they would be believed.

When we listen to children, we can listen to our own hurts and move to heal the brokenness we feel. When we believe children, we can believe in ourselves and can move out from behind the veil of denial and ignorance. When we value children, we can value ourselves and move toward others more openly and caringly. Perhaps when that begins to happen, the children who live in the narrow towns may grow up to become confident and competent adults.

5

Courage

The elevator door jerked open with a bang, startling its occupant almost as much as its occupant startled me. Large dark eyes stared steadily at the scene before them. Gingerly, the girl stepped off the elevator, escaping the impatient door, dragging a large paper shopping bag, tattered and faded coat sweeping behind her.

"This heah the kids' floor?" she demanded, of no one in particular.

That was how I met Flora. She was nine years old. Before our acquaintanceship ended, she taught me the meaning of courage.

"Sure. May I help you, honey?"

The charge nurse smiled, welcoming the defiant and fragile wisp with tightly braided pigtails.

"What's in your bag? You want help with your coat? Your daddy coming?"

The questions, skillfully asked, had an effect, for the bony little girl moved to the nurse's station and declared that she had secrets in the bag, was never parted from her coat, and " 'spected Papa any minute."

The next journey upward of the elevator did indeed bring Papa, along with the unmistakable odor of cheap whiskey. Too brightly, he greeted the girl and, as best he could, proceeded to check her into the care of our children's ward.

If she was aware of others' manner toward her father she gave no clue. Her admiration for him was obvious, and she responded brightly when he reached for her hand. Together, they followed the nurse's aide down the long antiseptic tunnel that swallowed them from view.

The end of my resident's training in pediatrics was near, and many thoughts occupied my mind. None, however, was able to push aside my interest in the thin pigtailed child with the ominous diagnosis. Although not directly responsible for cases that month, I managed to drop by every day, usually in the evening, to see how Flora was doing.

Rather well, at first.

She had, within a few days' time, assumed the duties of assistant ward secretary. "Dracula's office," she would answer the phone. "We don't want no blood today!"

New admissions were her charge and many an anxious, tearful child found comfort in her cheerful presence. She pretended to listen to their hearts with a much-too-large stethoscope and made faces at the lab technicians who came for blood samples. She seemed most interested in the happenings of others and paid scant attention to her own plight; even less, it seemed, as the blood counts and transfusions became more frequent.

"You all right?" I asked. She lay quietly on her bed, eyes half closed.

She nodded. "Just tired. I got leukeemie, you know."

"Yes, I know."

"Papa says I be's fine. He good to me, but he don't know much about being sick." She smiled thinly through crooked teeth, the conversation at an end.

She continued to be the focal point for the ward even though more and more of her time was spent in bed. The ruse of "seeing how Flora is" was transparent to all. What she was giving to the steady stream of those of us who came and went was acceptance. It became all right to hurt like children and be afraid and not know all the answers. Within Flora's world, there was no point in wasting time or energy on illusions of better things to come. Being was now, and reality was a smile and plenty of grits on the breakfast tray.

She was courage, and I learned how frail indeed a commodity it is.

Flora accepted us, delighted in our presence, and made us feel important. However, it was the sight of her father, older and tireder now, steps no longer swayed by alcohol, that lighted her eyes like the fire of an October sunset. As much as Flora accepted us, so did she adore her father. He who seemed to merit so little of our attention, painted stars in her soul and made her feel the vastness of life bursting at its seams. In him, she saw and experienced a dimension of love that was taught to us in the pulpit but rarely made its way past the church door. So strongly were we influenced by this love that there were whispers in our minds that she might be well and not die of her "leukeemie."

That, however, was simply not to be. Flora's illness took place before the tremendous strides in the chemotherapy of leukemia. In spite of our desperate attempts, she grew weaker, tireder, paler, and sicker. Still, her spirit persisted, and the flowers and gifts left for her turned up in the rooms of others "less fortunate."

Springtime came, and azaleas, and the circus. Clowns with painted faces visited the children's ward, bringing colorful balloons and ridiculous jokes. Flora loved it! She got a second wind; she screamed in delight at their comic predicaments and assumed an air of mock sympathy with those of sad countenance.

Flora, I thought, you will not give up or be left out, will you?

Her birthday was just a few days away, but a surprise party had been planned by the evening shift for the weekend before so her dad could be present. He came, dressed in his best, a large box under his arm. Her response to him was the complete openness, warmth, and delight we had come to expect. She saved his gift until last, and after the cake and ice cream had disappeared she opened the box. I had never seen her cry, but this time I thought she might. Certainly most of the rest of us had tears in our eyes. It was a clown doll: bright, colorful, and happy, a string of balloons tied to his hand. It was a goodbye and a beginning. She slept that night with the clown snuggled against her cheek, his happy eyes keeping a steady watch.

Weeks later, I found the clown, still smiling, where he had been placed after she died. He sits now, an invitation in his steady eyes, at the nurse's desk, waiting for the elevator to open so he can greet whoever is next in need of Flora's courage.

6

Hope

We had gone as far as the car would take us. The rest of the way, through half-frozen mud and tangled underbrush, was on foot. The parson, more confident than I, found a path, and in spite of my doubts and the cold, wet ooze my city shoes absorbed, we soon saw a cabin with lighted windows.

Someone had heard our approach, though no dog was around to announce our arrival, for the door swung open even before a greeting had been shouted. Little time was spent on introductions, even less on the reason for our visit. The parson and I were accepted by the cabin's occupants with no objections, and were warmed by the fitful heat from a kerosene stove.

With the "parson of the hills," I was there to deal with sickness where medical help was scarce and inconsistently sought. Although we were not many miles from my comfortable and well-equipped pediatric practice, I felt centuries removed. Here in my own state was another world, a world cloistered in coves and hollows, obscured from traveled highways, and screened from the world by lack of interest in its existence.

The flushed faces and weary eyes of the handful of children who lived in this particular patch of the world drew my attention immediately. Whatever used to separate them from me was now eliminated, and I was here in the now of their lives and at the center of their needs. Parson Kerry had brought some toys donated to his mission, which he presented. They were shiny and new, plastic-covered, the kind my children eliminated in a day. Soberly and without smiling, the children took the gifts, and, without removing the plastic containers, placed them on a shelf, nearly out of reach. The parson did not seem to notice but I caught him looking at me intently, urging me to keep silent.

Altogether, there were five children in the household, and that day four were sick. Fever, earaches, and one case of pneumonia consumed all the medicines I had brought. Fortunately, the antibiotics and cough syrups would remedy today's illnesses. About the next outbreak I could only speculate. I also wondered how, in spite of their illness, these children had forced their bodies to school that day. How had their tired minds withstood the monotony of a day at a desk? Or had they gone because the school had a government lunch program and their bodies needed the food of today more than their minds needed the thoughts that would prepare them for tomorrow?

I wondered.

Images of countries where I have worked as a part of medical mission teams came to mind. Was this very different? Were not poverty, marginal skills, and an isolated location producing the same effects that I had seen in other parts of the world? Were not the illnesses similar, the life span as short, and the helplessness as apparent as those in countries other than my own?

Discouraged and saddened, I felt the heat from the stove and its acrid fumes stifle my breath. I wanted to run, to escape this place, to avoid its children, to blot out any memory of its existence. I did not want to acknowledge and be defeated by this pocket of the third world in my own neighborhood. Why had the parson brought me here, where my few days' worth of medicines could do little to blot out a lifetime of deprivation? Trapped, my eyes sought the door, closed against winter, and willed it to open.

"You got any chewing gum, mister?"

About five, he asked the question cautiously, though with a grin that showed generous spaces between his upper teeth.

I jumped. Two of his sisters giggled, and a sense of relief came into the cabin.

Chewing gum made the rounds and I listened, drawn into their conversations in spite of myself.

"You know how fur it is to Jefferson!"

"Ain't no snakes now. Too cold!"

"How much that ear light cost?"

"You got any kids, mister doctor?"

"You gonna see Bessie McIntosh? She sick too."

Things went somewhat better after that. The aspirin was beginning to work and there was more animation in the children's faces, more spirit in their words. One of their toys, a homemade "whimmy diddle," came from a box filled with odd bits and pieces that encouraged their play more than the plastic-covered objects carefully set aside. Back and forth, back and forth, the stick moved over the notched wooden shaft, and the propeller whirled. I saw dreams of flight, the freedom of birds, and the delight of discovery in their play with a simple toy with a funny name. I also saw that one did not talk to poverty but to people, and the game the children played formed the words of the dialogue.

Beans and cornbread were the main fare for the evening meal. Surprisingly, it was not the parson who offered the blessing. Grandfather spoke. "Thank you, O God, for thy grace that gives us courage to look to the time when there will be no more hunger, or cold, or suffering, and no more death. Amen."

Hope. Pure and simple.

Trying to keep intact the island of warmth, someone closed the door quickly, ushering the two of us back into the cold. The mud had frozen solid, making walking easier. Fragments of cloud, glimpsed through creaking tree limbs, played hide and seek with the distant stars. Hurrying to keep stride with the parson, I wondered what I felt and why.

"They don't want charity and they don't want pity," the parson said. "Don't measure them as good or bad, rich or poor; just think of them as children. It's relationship, not position, that matters with them. You're uncomfortable because you think you ought to change their world, make things better. Maybe so. But whose is the better life? You judge their playing with a toy from the perspective of your children, and from what you think is right. Oh, don't get me wrong. Not for an instant do I think they should be denied proper food or medicine or anything else. But who prevents them from having it?"

We had reached the car, and I longed for the heater to warm me and stir the blood in my chilled hands and feet. If ever I come here again, I thought, I'll have sense enough to dress warmly.

If ever I come here again.

The parson was angry now, and I dared not interrupt, especially to complain about cold feet.

"I ask you again. Whose fault is it they are poor? Did God make them that way so we could have the token poor around to keep us pious?" He was thundering now, and I expected to be warmed by fire and brimstone.

The storm, however, was over. In our own way, we shared the silence. I thought about a whimmy diddle and children who liked to chew gum.

For a long time, we drove in silence. The hills dropped behind us and long stretches of road opened up ahead. Farmhouses slipped away into the darkness as the steadily increasing lights from the city gradually dulled the sparkle of the stars.

"No," I said as I got out of the car, my feet firmly striking the pavement of the driveway. "I don't think they are token poor, and I don't think God made them that way. I don't have many answers about poverty, but I guess I'll go again whenever you're ready."

He waved and accelerated toward the open road. Suddenly, he stopped and backed to where I stood, still watching.

"You'll need this, then. Catch."

Just in time, I grabbed the small object he hurled in my direction, a perfectly good package of my favorite chewing gum.

7

No Ordinary Child

"You want a boy or a girl?" I addressed the question to the lanky young man standing at my elbow. Awkwardly, his face partly covered by a surgeon's mask and his body swathed in a bulky green scrub suit, he tried to answer. Obviously, the gender of the child trying to be born mattered far less to him at the moment than the struggle his wife endured. For the last ten minutes, things had not gone well. Each new pain, and the command to "push," had been greeted by a determined effort, but to no avail. Exhaustion began to creep into the young woman's face. Beside me, her husband, voice trembling, offered words of encouragement, as much to himself as to her.

"What's wrong, Doc? Everything seemed to be going fine at first but I'm kinda scared now. Can't they do something?"

As if to answer his question, the obstetrician stood up, removed his gloves, and looked at both of us.

"Won't rotate," he said. "We'll have to section her."

Swiftly, the shrouded instrument table, sterile and waiting, was wheeled into place. The abdomen was cleaned and draped, anesthetic was administered, and the obstetrician-turned-surgeon, newly scrubbed and freshly gowned, opened his hand for the scalpel. Calmly, scrub nurse assisting, he cut through the layers of tissue, laying bare the rounded dome of the uterus with its precious cargo. A few moments more and a scrawny little face, topped by a thatch of dense black hair, emerged from the carefully placed incision. Nose and mouth were quickly suctioned and a raucous cry, accompanied by the intake of life's first breath, followed. As the rest of the baby girl's body was delivered, the reason for her failure to descend to the outside world became apparent.

Midway down her back, a large protrusion, covered with shiny membranes and filled with the coiled nerve cords intended for her lower body, lay ominous and waiting. Her legs, already thin and twisted, dangled helplessly as the nurse moved her quickly to the open resuscitator crib where I administered oxygen and assessed the damage. There were no problems with breathing; her cry was strong and the color of her skin excellent. She was perfect in every way— from the waist up.

I called her father, and he reluctantly left his sleeping wife to look with uncomprehending eyes at his daughter.

"There's a problem, Joe, and we'll need to talk. I'd rather wait until Sally is awake if that's all right with you."

He nodded assent and the baby and I proceeded to the special care nursery to cover the membranous sac with sterile solution and await the plan of attack.

Myelomeningocele, or spina bifida, is a condition known as a neural tube defect because the primitive nervous system, or neural tube, fails to form appropriately. This occurs, for unknown reasons, in the very early stages of intrauterine life. The location of the defect in the spine and the spinal cord determines the eventual level of function or performance of a child with the condition. A very low-lying protrusion— that is, one closest to the tail end of the backbone— will have the least effect on development and ability. The farther up the spine the protrusion is, the more serious the consequences, some protrusions being so high as to paralyze the chest and make breathing impossible. In such a case, the decision as to how to manage the treatment is not difficult. In all others, however, the boundaries are far less distinct and conclusions are less easily reached.

Fortunately, I had an hour or so, to think and to call in a neurosurgical colleague for consultation and help. In medical parlance, the lesion, we agreed, was high and not compatible with function of the legs, bowel, or bladder. Sensation below the level of the umbilical cord would be virtually absent. The decision to surgically close the large open sac, thereby saving her life, would need to be considered in the light of the parents' reactions and wishes as well as that of our own knowledge.

So we waited. Waited for the baby's mother, Sally, to awaken and for the group of parents, nurses, and doctors to form and to plan and to become a team. The time of Baby Doe regulations, which encourage anyone and everyone to give advice in making the decisions this couple faced, was still in the future. They would not be assailed by well-intentioned but misguided persons with no understanding of the problem seeking to pass judgment. Sally and Joe, facing a lifetime decision and dealing with the sadness and grief accompanying the loss of the normal child they had expected, would not have to hear the retorts and condemnations and cries of "murderer" flung at them that similar couples endure today. In this case, then, we were all fortunate. Whatever treatment choice was made, the decision could be reached through the best efforts of those who lived with and cared for this child and family, and no one else.

One thing bothered me. I did not know this family. Even though I addressed them by their first names, thereby hoping to lessen their anxiety about entering the strange hospital setting, I had only just met them. Their obstetrician, relying on some sixth sense about the progress of this pregnancy and knowing I was already in the hospital, had asked me to be present at the delivery. Sally and Joe were young, barely out of high school, from a small rural community, without friends or relatives present. They were here in the city, alone, for the birth of their child.

I did, however, remember Joe's reply to my question.

"I don't care if it's a boy or a girl, Doc, just so it's healthy."

So now I was apprehensive about what was to come, what their doctor and I needed to tell them, and how they would react.

I worried needlessly. Their answer was simple and yet profound.

"Do what you can to fix her. She's ours and we aim to raise her the best way we know how."

They named her April. Her life was not long, for she succumbed to the complications of her disorder before she reached her fifth birthday. During that time she imprinted herself permanently on all of us who occupied her world. She never walked, nor did she say any words except maybe "mama" or "dada." She had no need to do so. She commanded with an energy that was as purposeful and directed as if it were planned from the beginning of time. For all I knew, perhaps it had been. Whatever the case, I learned and observed two things in those five years. April promoted growth in her parents that was barely short of miraculous, and she made me know that I, with my medical wisdom and great storehouse of advice, was tolerated only because I was available.

April recovered quickly from surgery and waited impatiently for Sally to do the same. Wisely, Sally took her time, for she had much to learn. With April's lead, she discovered the best position for diapers to keep April's hips properly aligned, the most appropriate times for satisfying April's ravenous appetite, and when holding and rocking were desired instead of sleep.

On going-home day, April sported a tiny pink bow

taped to her hair. The main attraction, however, was a large pacifier on which she chewed noisily and with much satisfaction. When I attempted to remove it to complete her discharge examination, she clamped down defiantly, arched her back, and blazed away with indignant eyes. I retreated. Satisfied, she settled back into her crib and waited for her parents to receive final instructions, goodbyes, and good-luck wishes. I could still hear her noisy enjoyment of the pacifier as they rounded the corner and disappeared from sight.

Not for a moment do I believe that children like April are destined to be born to certain families, either as punishment or reward. I do not believe in the kind of God who would champion such interference. What I do believe is that a kind of grace is available that fosters the will and stimulates the ability of those in such a setting to move into a plane of life that enlarges them and enriches others. I also believe that the vehicle of that grace is most often the very child who appears initially to be the stumbling block for the whole family. Like the character in the Chinese language that stands for both danger and opportunity, such children occupy a point in time that offers, to perceptive souls, some risk and great adventure.

April came presenting that option. I wondered how it would be received.

The first return visit to the office was routine. Protesting my invasion of her space before she was ready, April permitted my examination with reluctance. The pacifier, already showing signs of wear, I elaborately ignored, only to snatch it unceremoniously out of her mouth when she yawned. Exam completed, I offered it back. Mouth closed tightly, she refused. Round one still belonged to April.

Joe and Sally observed my discomfort and laughed aloud. They had both come for the visit, a pattern which, happily, continued. They seemed pleased with April's decisive manner and told me they had taken her to church for everyone to see. The small yellow flower pinned to Sally's blouse had been a gift honoring their new child. She obviously wore it with pride.

Judging from the neatness of April's appearance and the well-cared-for scar on her back, Sally was exhibiting mothering and nursing skills greater than I had expected.

"You're doing very well with her care. Is there anything you need help with?"

She responded to my question by reaching into a large cloth bag and handing me a book.

"Joe got some overtime last week, and he found this for me in a secondhand bookstore over on Hanover Street. The pictures explain what the writing is saying. It's helped me a lot." She flushed with pleasure at her accomplishment.

The book, an illustrated guide to skilled nursing care, was not new, but its information was sound. I was truly surprised and said so.

"Well," Joe drawled, "April ain't exactly an ordinary child, and we aim to do all we can to take care of her, just like I said."

That was the phrase I had searched for in my own thinking about April, particularly after the pacifier caper in the hospital.

"Joe," I said, "you are indeed right. There is nothing at all ordinary about this child, nothing at all."

Throughout her first year of life, April gained weight slowly. She was admitted to the hospital for the placement of a shunt to relieve pressure from obstructed spinal fluid, and again for the treatment of a kidney infection. Undaunted, pacifier ready, she smiled her way through such adventures and gained a following of sorts among the hospital staff.

Likewise the mother. There was a happy spring to her step as she walked around the ward, dropping in on other mothers, relieving them of their watch, and promoting a gentle interchange of ideas that seemed to make the days shorter and the nights more restful. At home, she wheeled April around in a little red wagon, often stopping to talk to other children about why it was that her daughter couldn't walk. I wasn't surprised to learn that Joe had worked his way up to shift supervisor and with his extra salary had paid the first installment on Sally's tuition to the community college school of nursing. April, not being very ordinary, stimulated that kind of growth in people.

The second winter of April's life brought trouble. She fought pneumonia, ate poorly, and her legs, thin and bony, stiffened and twisted on her tiny frame. Each illness seemed to tire her more, and I feared the worst. Still, she pulled into spring, pacifier chewed to a dog-eared remnant, her temper poised, ready to pounce if I misjudged her mood.

A summer trip to the beach greatly renewed her energy and when I next saw her there was no mistaking the fact that she planned to be around awhile yet no matter what I thought. She proved that point quite definitely just a few weeks later.

Pneumonia, accompanied this time by shallow breathing and a slowing pulse, brought her to the children's ward once again. Her temperature dropped to well below normal and the spots of color on her cheeks faded. For a long time I stood by her bed, watching the slow drip of the IV match the movement of her chest. Her eyes remained closed and I was certain that this time her valiant struggle would end.

As reassuringly as possible, I spoke to Sally and Joe. "Here is my home number. You may need me before the night is over."

Understanding, they merely nodded. April must have heard my voice, for her eyes flickered open for a moment, then, seeing me, closed again.

Surprisingly, my sleep was not interrupted. Curious, I made my first stop on morning rounds at April's room. She waited for me with eyes snapping in triumph, furiously chewing her pacifier and obviously telling me once again that she, not I, would decide when it was time for her to leave.

Eventually she did move on, but not before Sally wore her nurse's pin, and a son, full of life and quite complete, brought the gift of another yellow flower. Just to be sure, I pocketed the pacifier placed in his crib. After all, one extraordinary child in that family was about all I could handle.

8

Monsters

Monday morning, and knee-deep in winter, too. Fussing at myself for forgetting my umbrella and dripping from the results of that error, I sought to reach the safety of my office, where I would be unseen and unquestioned. No problem. Judging from the laughter coming from the laboratory, the office staff was engaged in merriment much too rich for them to be concerned about someone as soggy and bedraggled as I.

"What's this, now?" I tried to bluff my way into being stern. My empty coffee cup and hair plastered to my glasses only added to their amusement.

"Aren't there patients to see, phones to answer, and charts to file? I mean, after all, this is a serious place, you know."

But the Scrooge approach didn't work either, so I gave up, filled my cup, and waited.

"You know all that talk about how impressionable babies are and how you try to get parents to develop a sense of what their child is like?" Maggie asked. Maggie was the nurse.

I nodded, not sure of what was coming.

"Well, Mrs. Abrams called about Seth. She's the mother who wants to raise the most psychologically secure person ever. It seems, however, that each time she changes his diaper, he 'baptizes' her full force. She wanted to know if it would hurt his psyche if she directed his efforts toward the wall instead of her face!"

General round of laughter. I managed a smile too.

"You think that's funny?" Beth, our lab assistant, had another story. "You know why I didn't get a urine specimen Friday from that boy who was the last regular physical we did? Well, I didn't want to embarrass him by sending his mother to the bathroom with him, so I told him how to use the specimen bottle and then said to bring it to me. He did fine, except after filling the specimen bottle, he flushed it and brought me the empty container!"

Laughter. Not bad medicine, actually. Now warmer and drier, I felt that maybe I could manage Monday morning after all. Somewhere in each new young patient lurked one more smile, if only we knew where to find it.

That is why I was completely unprepared for what happened next.

The complaint written on the chart waiting on the examining room door simply said *Earache*. Good, I thought. That will speed things up a bit. Opening the door, I noticed immediately that Jared was crouched in the corner, his back jammed against the exam table, arms securely wrapped around one of its legs.

"I want to die," he said.

His mother did not move, only stared at me and waited.

Jared repeated his words, his voice flat and tired. "I want to die."

The laughter in me died, and I saw no smiles as I tried to look into this child. "What's happening?" I managed to stammer.

"I don't know. He's been that way for two days now. Won't eat, won't sleep, just jabbers 'I want to die, I want to die!'"

I thought for a brief moment that Jared's mother was going to start screaming. She breathed rapidly. Gradually, though, she began to gain control of herself.

I approached Jared slowly, watching how fiercely he clung to the table, seeing his face frozen like a mask, sensing his fear.

"He's scared to death," I said without thinking. Of course, I reasoned; what else?

I sat down on the floor a few feet away and began to play with a toy left in the room. As soon as Jared showed the first sign of relaxing, I gently pushed the toy to him. Minutes passed before finally, tentatively, he reached for the object and held it, his eyes fixed on me all the while.

"Monster," he said. "Monster's going to get me!"

Without warning, he threw the toy with all his strength, smashing it against the wall behind his mother. Instinctively, she and I both ducked, alarmed at his action, confused by his words.

His outbursts seemed to have a calming effect, for he did not reattach himself to the table. Instead, he sat, eyes pleading, looking at me.

"What has happened to scare him so?" I asked, turning to the young woman while still keeping one eye on her son.

She hesitated and paled slightly.

"It's the TV, I guess," she said at last. "That monster comedy show. He watches it every day. You know the one I mean? It's about a family of people who act like Frankenstein monsters."

I could not honestly say I knew the one she meant. A comedy didn't sound too terrifying, but how does a four-year-old know the difference? The lines that separate his knowledge of what is real and what is fantasy are wavy and indistinct. Dreams become reality, monsters lurk beneath the kitchen sink, and what the television presents seems believable. For Jared and for other children his age, magic operates the world. The sun comes up in the morning tugged into the light of day by a giant with an enormous fishhook shaped like an anchor. Vacuum cleaners have secret ways of whooshing everything, including little kids, into their bellies, and stars are shot into the sky each night to light the way for a band of elves on their way to work.

These thoughts are amusing when recalled as childhood memories. It's reassuring, too, to know that even when we're too old to believe that giants and elves are afoot, the sun still shines and stars continue to twinkle.

"Jared, can you draw me a picture of a monster?"

He responded by scribbling on a piece of paper, eventually drawing a circle with a mouth and eyes.

"That's it. I don't like the monster. I want to go home." He looked at me matter-of-factly and walked to the door. His mother followed.

"I guess I'll change the TV channel more often. Looks like he's OK now. Thanks for your help." With Jared in the lead, they left.

Dumbfounded, I sat on the floor, searching for pieces of the broken toy.

"Mmm," Maggie said. "There are other toys I can get for you if you need to take a break!" She stood by the open door, surveying my situation and shaking her head.

"Did you see Jared?" I asked, ignoring her pointed comments. "Something is badly wrong there, and he was trying to tell me what it was, but, confound it, I've missed the whole message. It is certainly possible that the TV program is scaring him badly, but I would not have expected such an abrupt change in his behavior if that were so. He seemed to be out of control and calculating at the same time. Maggie, please call them tomorrow and see how he is."

Concerned for Jared, she agreed, and we went back to the job of tackling Monday, a task now grown to challenging proportions.

Even with the many happenings of that cold, wet, wintry day, I could not push thoughts of Jared aside. When all the patients had been seen and treated, I asked Maggie if she knew much about the family.

"She's a single mother. Used to have a job as a secretary, but she left the place for the work phone number blank when she filled out today's register. She looked harassed and jittery to me. But that's normal, I guess, for someone whose child is crying that he wants to die."

The telephone interrupted our conversation, and Maggie went to answer it. When she hung up, she turned with a smile.

"End your day on a positive note. The Hawkinses have a new baby girl and all is well."

I smiled, pleased for the Hawkinses, then turned off the office lights and, umbrella firmly in hand, faced the wet darkness of a winter evening.

By the time I reached home, a dull ache had settled in my neck and a scratchy throat added to my discomfort and probably accounted in part for my irritability.

"Will you please turn that TV down! Oh, never mind, I'll do it myself."

Scowling at the boys, I reached for the switch, only to stop and stare.

"What's this show?" I asked.

"The Happy Monster Hour," came the reply.

So, I thought. This is what terrifies children and makes four-year-old boys want to die.

I was not impressed. The "monsters" were funny caricatures of people, like clowns, and the situations of the story seemed harmless, set in the atmosphere of a living room that was basically ordinary if a bit eccentric. Still, I mused, imagination can embellish even the tamest of events so as to make them vibrate with terror. And imagination, I knew, was a four-year-old child's middle name.

Aspirin helped my cold symptoms. Still, I slept fitfully that night. Toward morning I struggled awake from a dream in which I was a small boy running from clouds full of giant faces waiting to devour me.

"Scared to death," I said aloud.

Through the bedroom window, dawn's light seeped past the curtains, slowly driving the clouds of fear back into the harmless and playful patterns on the wall. Fear, I thought, is a marvelous weapon. In my adult world, used judiciously, it helps avoid danger and enhances appropriate dependence on others. It is a defense against foolish expression and a force to mobilize one to action. Yet fear may also be a stumbling block, a creeping paralysis that strangles the instinct for self-preservation. In the minds of children, fear may well be a valuable emotion that challenges their investigation of imagination and forces them ultimately to bet on the side of what is real. That kind of fear is life-giving, and, I suspect, judiciously encouraged by parents whose own caution is a buffer and whose fear is held in check by the discipline of their years.

But what of Jared and his mother? Who was the buffer, who possessed the years of discipline to protest, and against what or whom were the protests rightly directed? Not, I felt certain, a TV program with a monster routine of stale and predictable jokes.

"That's not much evidence to go on," the social worker from the Protective Services Division said when I telephoned.

"I know," I said, then paused to marshal my thoughts. "Call it a hunch, but that boy was telling me something. I think he knew his mother was in danger. I think he feared for her life, not his own."

"Have it your way, then. I have to be in that end of town on another call, so I'll make a home visit this morning. I'll get back to you, either way, this afternoon."

It was late in the day when she called, from the downtown police station.

"It's a long story, sad, but not unusual," she said. "You were right. Jared's mother had allowed a friend, or someone she thought was a friend, to move in with them. She quit her job since he seemed willing to support them. Soon afterward she became aware of his drinking, and then she became the target of his vicious drunken rages. Miraculously, Jared was unharmed, but as you suspected, he was afraid for his mother's life. His plea to you was in the only language he felt safe to use. A lot smarter than you'd think for four, isn't he? When I arrived at their house today, I was just in time to call for police help. They're safe now. The man has been charged with assault, and I'm taking Jared and his mom to the bus station. They're going back to her family to get some perspective and a fresh start, away from the danger of any more attacks."

I listened, the warmth of relief spreading through the aching cold of my muscles.

"One other thing," she said before hanging up. "Jared said to tell you 'bye."

So the four-year-old, with strength and discipline beyond his years, had channeled his fear and made it the weapon his mother had been unable to use. For a little while yet, however, I hoped he would not have to be so old. Rather, I hoped he could chase his playmates in a rousing game of "Find the Monster" and watch the stars being born at night. Maybe, I thought, if he was lucky enough, he would catch sight of just one of the elves, hurrying to catch his mates, trying not to be late for work.

9

Anger

September breezes directed the first leaves of fall
to the playground. First- and second-graders, their
pent-up energy unleashed, played as if determined to
capture all the moments their break allowed. A game
of kickball, hotly contested, occupied the center of
the playground and most of the children. A few, forgetting advice to the contrary, searched, barefoot, for
crawdads and other treasures in the tiny creek bor-
dering the playground. It was another group, however, mostly girls, running in a circle, their colorful
skirts and blouses like the tapestry of leaves above
them, that caught my attention.

Around the circle they went, then, hands clapping
in rhythm, they moved toward its center, counting:

"One, two, buckle my shoe.
Three, four, shut the door."

For a moment, the years melted and I remembered
recess time: dusty, hot playgrounds, water gulped
thirstily from a collapsible aluminum cup, marbles
shot across lines drawn in the dust, and the way we
too learned to count.

"Five, six, pick up sticks," I joined, and the girls
giggled, embarrassed and pleased.

Happily, I thought, some parts of ourselves keep
happening.

Black bag in hand, I entered the school, waved to

the office secretary, and walked down the hall with the squeaky floor to Mrs. Stevens' fifth grade class. Today I was show-and-tell for Jennifer, who had asked me if I would talk to her class about what it's like to be a doctor for children.

It's a mixture of many things, of course, some funny, some sad, all enriching. What I wanted to share with them was the enthusiasm of feeling a kinship with their youth without damaging the image of doctors as people they could trust. Some humor and some facts, mixed with honesty and straight answers to their questions, would be the format.

"What's in the black bag?" I already knew John, who had asked the question. He lived in my neighborhood and was not the least bit awed by the mystery of a doctor's little black bag.

"Well, I'm glad you asked. Very important things. Let me show you."

I had planned for this, knowing someone would ask. I didn't want to get too technical too soon. Reaching into the bag, I pulled out a pair of socks.

"In case my feet get wet." I grinned. "Now here's my lunch, and then there's always a quarter for a phone call. You know, in case I'm late."

Laughter came from several who remembered what their parents always said about being prepared to call home if they were going to be late.

Finally, I reached for a shiny, large, red apple, and placed it on the desk in front of me.

"Why an apple?" I asked.

"To keep the doctor away!"

The stage was set. Jennifer's show-and-tell went well. I passed around tongue blades, allowed them to listen to one another's hearts, and showed them how to look into one another's ears. They did indeed ask many questions, and I found myself challenged to keep up.

"How many bones does a person have?"

"What happens if your brain is messed up and you write backwards?"

"Why is it that you have a cold when you really feel hot?"

"How come I got mono and I never kissed anybody?"

Too quickly, the hour drew to a close. As I packed up I saved the apple for last. "What shall I do with this?" I asked.

"Eat it," came a chorus of answers.

"Great," I responded. "Healthy food keeps the body running, but keeping the doctor away is not always a good idea."

Mrs. Stevens walked with me to the office. She was proud of her class, of their questions and their eager interest to know new things.

"Well," she said, "thanks. They may not all grow up to be doctors, but at least they won't feel so vulnerable and unprepared when they need to visit one."

I thought suddenly again of learning to count, and of those shutting doors in the rhyme. The enthusiasm in Mrs. Stevens' classroom was enough to encourage the interest and hard work of those adults who try to open the doors of adventure for children ready to step through them.

"Doctor." The secretary interrupted my thoughts. "Your office called. They need to talk with you." She pointed to the phone on her desk.

"Sorry," Maggie said, "but there's a problem that can't seem to wait until morning—a three-year-old boy who won't stay in his room at night and whose parents are serious about their desperation. You're scheduled to see them at four o'clock."

Doors and drat, I thought. Just tell them to shut their door! The phone, however, was already silent, and I had no choice but to give up the idea of getting off early that day.

Maggie must truly have suspected an urgent need, and as I sat across from the Barbers and listened to their story unfold, I mentally agreed with Maggie's concern.

"We have been married three months. Chris is my child from my first marriage." The boy's mother sat, rigid and unblinking, her speech clear and sharp. Were it not for the pain obvious in her eyes, I would have judged her to be as rigid as her posture. She continued. "We have had it with Chris. I don't believe in violence, but I have resorted to spanking him for almost everything he does. Today I reached for a belt and realized that I—we—need help. Can you, please, help us?"

More than a plea, a statement, or a question, it was a release. She made no effort to check the tears, nor did she take her eyes off her son, who sat, legs crossed, chin braced, next to her husband.

"Last week, friends came to visit." Paul Barber spoke. "Chris grabbed one of my golf clubs and literally chased them out of the house. But the worst thing of all is that he will not sleep in his own bed. We beg, bribe, threaten, and scream, but he ends up sleeping with us every night. Doctor, we have been married only three months, but I don't have to tell you the honeymoon is definitely over."

The bitterness in his voice was undisguised. Maggie was right. These folks were desperate. Hard to believe the source of all this, and the focus of resentment, was a thirty-five-pound creature known as a three-year-old boy.

For a while, I sat listening, waiting to hear more if anyone wanted to speak. The silence had not become awkward before Chris broke it with a laugh.

"Boy, did they run! Next time I'll throw rocks!"

His mother gripped the sides of her chair. I knew she was right to fear using the belt. Chris was a lightning rod waiting to be struck with the storm he was igniting. Drastic measures were needed and I thought furiously about how best to initiate them.

On a hunch, I reached into the bag I had carried with me from the school, retrieved the apple, and held it toward Chris. "You like red?"

He had not expected that; my offer provided an opening wedge and I quickly continued.

"How many people live in your house?"

"Just me and Mommy, that's all!" He hurled the words defiantly toward me, all the while looking at his stepfather.

"Do your friends like red too?" I asked. He did not answer, and I felt him close the small opening the two of us had shared. Still, I was satisfied. What he had said provided a clue to the confusion and hurt that had generated his anger. I would follow that clue, but not now.

"Here, Chris, take the apple home with you. I need a friend to share red things with and I'm glad you like it."

I half expected him to grab the apple and throw it, so deeply was he controlled by his hostility. For a moment he hesitated, then settled back, the shiny red apple clenched tightly in his hands.

"Seems that things are on edge a great deal at your home now." Deliberately, I softened the tone of my response, not wanting to add to the agitation or resentment of any one person in the family. Speaking clearly so that Chris could not fail to hear my recommendation, I continued.

"I'd suggest you take first things first. Chris is fortunate to have his own room, so let's make sure he is allowed to enjoy it when he needs to sleep. Tonight, after you have read him a story, encouraged him to talk about the day, and shared your prayer or thoughts with him, say good night. Mean it. Tell Chris you will hear him if any problems need your help so that he will not need to come searching for you or stay with you. Do not close his door. Close yours. You need privacy, and that is appropriate."

I stood, bringing the meeting to a close.

"Please make an appointment to see me next week. I'll want some time to visit with Chris alone as well as to speak with you."

"Chris," I said, turning to face the youngster, "would you please bring some of your toys next time you visit with me? Perhaps we could have some time to play with them together."

I smiled at everyone in a reassuring and professional manner. I felt my advice would work, but I sensed their anxiousness and doubt about my suggestions. I hoped fervently that they would have the strength to try them anyway.

As if to answer my unspoken hope, Mr. Barber turned in the doorway and said, "We've tried so many things, one more won't hurt us."

The office was quiet after that, and I wandered to the window to look outside. How peaceful fall seemed. Its clear blue sky, soft winds, and colorful leaves formed a scene that seemed ripe for rocking chairs and long, thoughtful walks. How is it we humans seem so unable to catch the rhythm that such days offer? How is it a boy like Chris can be so explosive and damaging to himself and his family, in spite of the peace they want for him?

Maggie ushered me out, locking the office door behind her. "I had a friend once whose three-year-old refused to sleep by herself," she remarked. "They had quite a struggle convincing her that she could be safe in her own room at night."

"This is different, Maggie. In addition to the normal fear of unknown things that imaginative three-year-old children experience, Chris is dealing with some pretty deep issues. I constantly marvel at the strength of children and the resources they possess to shape both the circle of whatever makes up their world and the people in it. Ordinarily, fears at this age simply guarantee the extra protection or reassurance children perceive they need. Once satisfied, they move with their families to the next plateau of life. Chris possesses enormous strength; however, there are no boundaries to help him to define it. He is as frightened by his own power as he is by his false perception that his mother is abandoning him for someone else. It will take more than an apple to remedy this situation, Maggie!"

Appointment time came, but the Barbers did not arrive. No one answered their phone when we called to inquire. My heart sank. Maybe shutting the door had not been such a good idea after all.

The next morning, however, they did call, to apologize for missing their visit and to reschedule.

"That's funny," Maggie said. "She told me they had gone to the park and were having such a good time they simply forgot about coming to see you."

Well, I thought, something is working, to get results that quickly.

Chris, as encouraged, brought some of his favorite toys. Vigorously and with appropriate noises, he ran his toy cars up and down the carpet, careening them off the end of the bookshelf. Soon tired of that game, he followed my lead as I offered blocks, large white buttons, and some bottle caps.

"Build me a house, Chris, and show me your room."

With elaborate style, which I had suspected he possessed in abundance, Chris formed the blocks to create an image of his home. Bottle caps and buttons became the different people who lived in it and the friends who came to visit. After that, he needed only an occasional hint from me to tell a story. Frustration and anger surfaced as he worked through the terror he had felt when his mother had gone away for her "wedding trip" and the cold empty feeling that remained when she returned. Doubting he could trust her and suspecting that his new stepfather had deliberately taken her from him, he had resorted to means he felt necessary for survival. Suddenly, he struck the blocks with his hand, and they scattered across the room, his anger thus well demonstrated.

I did not interfere. He needed to express his feelings and this was a way, acceptable and healing, for him to do it. He and I would play many such games before this power before us was in harmony with his growth, not in opposition to it.

"Thank you for bringing your toys, Chris. Next time let's draw pictures, OK?"

"I don't know how to draw," he replied.

"Then I'll share a secret with you that will help you learn. Now I want to talk with your mom and dad. Will you be all right playing with other boys and girls while you wait?"

He nodded. His mother smiled brightly as Chris passed his parents in the hall.

"So things are better, I take it?"

"Much better," they agreed.

His mother continued. "He tried only once to get in our room. We told him we were all right and he was safe, and he went back to his bed. We don't even have to close our door now, and it's been less than a week."

"That adds to my opinion of Chris," I said. "He is a very bright and determined boy. He is angry and he is afraid. The strange thing is, closing the door helped him to understand that you were in charge and he doesn't have to be. That was very reassuring to him and immediately lessened his fear. I would like to suggest some other things to do as well, and I want you to talk together about what is happening as the result of your new marriage. Chris may not understand all you say, but he will feel that you are including him and that's what he really wants."

Chris and I spent several hours together over the next two months, playing, building, and learning to draw. His anger dissolved into silly jokes and bright-colored pictures, and when he began to spend more time telling me about what "me and Dad did," I knew he had reached the next plateau. In future times, when anger would be needed, I trusted that he would confidently direct its power, not be its victim.

Another inviting and friendly fall, regal in scotch-plaid splendor, had rolled around when the Barbers unexpectedly paid me a visit.

"We just came for a moment," Paul said. "I've been transferred, and we're moving soon. We wanted to say goodbye—all of us, especially Chris."

Chris, bigger, hair neatly brushed, hands behind his back, stepped from behind his parents.

"Thanks for showing me how to draw. Here's a present for you. Now you can have something red to keep."

It was a picture of a large red apple. In the corner, with his mother's help, he had written, "A friend."

10

Grief

"Supper?"

"Hmm." Preoccupied with orders for a late-afternoon admission, I barely heard the invitation. Becky, color rising slightly in her cheeks and brown unruly curls brushing against her starched white collar, tried again. This time I listened more closely.

"Could you maybe—uh, come and have supper with me?"

Down the hall a young teenager called loudly for her supper, and the cart full of food trays rattled past the nurse's station, so that I had to pause before answering.

"I wanted to say thanks for helping me," she said.

"OK. Sure. How about Thursday night? I'm not on call then."

Relieved, she agreed Thursday was a good time, and so it was decided. I would be her guest for dinner, in her newly acquired apartment: a housewarming of sorts.

"Thanks for the invitation. Any questions on those orders, beep me."

The week, cool and damp for late spring, passed amid a flurry of seasonal viruses and early camp physicals. Thursday was full, and some perplexing problems had arisen that kept me preoccupied. Even so, I did not forget Becky's invitation, and, only a few minutes late, I pulled into the parking lot of her apartment building.

Memory would not disclose how long I had known her. Somehow I recalled an energetic, knobby-kneed, thin-chested little girl, who coughed all the time but never complained. In the transition from childhood to adolescence, she crossed the line from patient to friend, and then her battles, furiously fought, became my own. She endured frequent hospitalizations, recurrent pneumonia, creeping loss of weight, and vanished time for play and friends. She planned for other times in other places. With a persistence born of stubbornness and fueled by a desire to be responsible, she pushed on through high school and landed a job as a ward secretary for the pediatric floor. There, she was no stranger.

Drawing cool damp air into my lungs, I remembered that she spoke of spring as her favorite season.

"Flowers, you know, and new things coming alive. Easter and all that stuff. Makes me think, Hey, life, let's go one more round anyway, just for the fun of it!"

Spring for her also meant a respite from the constant threat of another bout with pneumonia, and I half expected that was the real reason she breathed in its fragrance so joyfully.

The apartment was modern sterility, but she had succeeded in adding warmth with some pictures and with a colorful afghan her grandmother had knitted. The dining table was covered with a carefully laid cloth, and two places, one at either end, were set.

I congratulated her on her efforts and presented her with a small gift, which she placed on the entry table next to photos of her family and a snapshot of a young man unknown to me.

"He's in the young people's group at church, and he wants me to go with them for their beach trip this year. He's nice. You'd like him. I hope I can get off work early; I'd like to go."

What she meant was, I'd like to go if I'm well enough.

Green peas, meat loaf, iced tea (already sweetened),

milk and flour gravy, and real biscuits: Southern. Later
I remembered that meal well, and especially how it
tasted. The meat was dry and crusty, the peas
scorched, the tea too sweet, the gravy lumpy, and the
biscuits doughy. Funny thing, though; for years I have
recalled that last supper we shared as one of the tasti-
est meals of my life. She made it that way, just as from
the weakness of her illness she provided a window
through which I could see her strength.

"How many kids in your practice have CF?" She
tried not to cough as she talked. Cystic fibrosis. Unre-
lenting evil, faceless monster, windmill for Quixotes
like me. Her brother had already fallen prey to it, but
she held it at bay, thereby teaching those like me, often so slow to learn, what it means to live in the eter-
nity of now.

"Several. Why do you ask?"

"Do you go to their funerals when they die?"

Not exactly truthfully: "Yes. Most of the time. I'm
pretty busy, you know."

"Will you come to mine?"

"Sure." But the question isolated me in a corner of
discomfort, and my answer was given with eyes
averted. Where Becky was leading me I could not say.
I sensed she was teaching faster than I wanted to
learn.

"It won't be for me, you know. I won't be there. I'll
be somewhere else. Heaven. Something. I haven't
gotten it all figured out yet." She thought for a moment. "Seems it's supposed to be a place, but more
and more I think it's an idea about how we get along
with each other—and God too, I guess."

She paused, her eyes looking beyond me, as if
watching a thought become visible. I dared not speak.
I sensed she saw a vista I could not see, a place where,
for now at least, I could not go.

"That's it," she said at last. "Heaven isn't a place at
all, not like we think of places, at any rate. It's a
relationship."

I watched the concentration in her face relax and felt just a twinge of envy for not sharing fully what she had just discovered.

She turned to me, in the present once more. "That's not what I started to tell you. I want you to go to my funeral because you need to be there. It isn't such a bad thing, to feel sad and cry and miss someone who was your friend. That's a good way to say good-bye. Clean, clear, like being on top of a hill when the sun sets and the breeze of evening stirs the tops of tall oak trees. Lots of times I've listened to the doctors when they have a patient who is really bad sick. Sounds funny, I guess, but they're scared too, just like the rest of us. Sometimes, when one of the really sick kids dies, they get pretty upset. At times, they are very sympathetic, but I've noticed too many who just want to go away and leave everything to the chaplain. I can tell the ones who are too scared to go to the funeral. They get snappy, look tired, and talk too much. They discuss every angle of the case with their doctor friends, hoping to be told that their treatment was correct. Unfortunately, they don't seem reassured, even though their care was the most modern and exact that could possibly be given."

She stopped to cough and to drink from a cup of water.

So, I thought. You've learned a lot about us. You know how we fear making mistakes, about the sense of vulnerability we are ashamed to admit, and you have seen how reluctantly we face death, which we don't think could be caused by anything apart from personal error or cosmic failure.

"I wouldn't want to see you snappy, and I don't like it when you talk too much. So do yourself a favor; go to my funeral."

Another coughing seizure, then she continued.

"It will be easier for you to face your other patients with CF, cancer, or whatever else they have. They'll know if you start to avoid them, or cut short your visits, or talk about stupid things. They want you to be what you say you are, what you try to be; a friend. And friends," she said very carefully, "stick together to the very end."

She didn't want any help with the dishes, reinforcing her claim to autonomy. Her smile ushered me into the night air, perfumed by freshly blooming honeysuckle. She breathed deeply of the romantic fragrance, and I think she was already longing to turn from the place where we were to the relationship she had envisioned.

"Thank you, Becky. For the dinner and the lesson. And, uh, yes. I'll be there. You can count on it."

The real food of the dinner had been a multiple-star gourmet feast. Her teaching did help. No longer did I try to remain immune from the grief of those who sought my help. Sharing in that grief did not weaken me, as I had feared, but gave me courage to be honest about my frustration and accept the anger and hurt of those who were in pain, as necessary, and not as a judgment. I could see, born of Becky's dying, a new dimension to living. Here was a new understanding of my role as a physician, a role that called on me to bridge the gap between living and dying with reality and acceptance, pushing back the fear and denial so often present. I understood what she was saying about relationships. Sharing grief and the fear of the unknown together, comfort emerged, and I knew that neither I nor the children I treated would ever again face the emptiness of death alone.

It was not the warmth of spring and the explosion of colors she preferred, or perhaps even deserved, but the cool crisp air of early December when I gathered with many others to acknowledge Becky's passing. Words, well spoken, of compassion and hope, were offered. Tears were shed and memories of earlier days and playful times, especially those with Becky at the center, were revived. In spite of the pain we felt and the loss we had experienced, an occasional smile could be seen as we stood among the stone markers. There was no denying the fact that this, in addition to being a goodbye, was a celebration—a celebration in recognition of a person who valued and created relationships.

The fading sun cast the long shadows of the neatly spaced headstones across the brown grass, which rustled as gusts of wind swept unhindered around those of us gathered by the graveside. After a while, goodbyes given to the wind, we too began to scatter like the dry leaves beneath our feet.

I missed Becky already and felt a bit cheated by her absence. Even so, a smile came unbidden as I recalled our supper together. I don't think she would have minded in the least that I hurried to catch the others, to invite them to join me in sharing a good Southern meal, complete with homemade gravy and biscuits.

11

Gifts

I ran into him in the gift shop, searching for cards.
"Merry Christmas," he said.
"Happy Hanukkah," I replied. "How goes everything?"
"Well," he responded. So we chatted, catching up on small details that were to us significant, keeping alive our friendship in the midst of busy times.
"You should see Jeffrey." He beamed. "Three years old and bursting with growth."
I laughed. The way he came alive when he spoke of his son, revealing himself in total openness, was a great gift and I treasured it, as I knew others had.
"Well, now, what's his latest accomplishment?" I asked in a bantering tone.
My friend became quiet and a distant look settled into his eyes. "It's about Christmas," he said. "Jeffrey asked about it the other day. We told him about the holiday, why we celebrated it differently, and about the giving of gifts. He was especially curious about the Salvation Army and their collection of money for the poor. Yesterday we decided to go for dinner and to shop. As we got into the car, I noticed he had brought his piggy bank. I told him he probably would not need it, but he insisted. When we got to the shopping center, he hopped out and made his way quickly to the nearest Salvation Army volunteer. I caught up with him just in time to hear him

say, in his best three-year-old manner, 'This is my gift, too.' "

For several moments, overcome by what had taken place, neither of us spoke. Finally, with a warm hand-clasp and wishes to be remembered to each other's families, we parted. I watched the joy in his stride as he pushed through the crowd, and thought for a moment that I too could see through the window of Jeffrey's childhood the marvelous gift he had shared with us all.

12

Why Me, Lord?

"Fifteen next week," she replied to my question about her age.

"Ellie, you seem so grown up. I always think of you as waiting for me to make the first move, gritting your teeth for those inevitable shots, and not volunteering much conversation without being asked. Now, you don't even look like that little girl."

Ellie, her pretty face surrounded by soft wispy curls, glanced at me, smiled, and waited. She had asked her mother to stay home; she wanted to see me alone. A sign of growing up, of wanting to make her own decisions, I thought. As she sat there, though, I realized that the first move was still up to me.

"How may I help you, Ellie?" No complaint had been written on her chart, just *Wants to see doctor*.

"My stomach has been bothering me. I think I have a virus or something."

She didn't look at me as she spoke. I wondered if there were problems in school. I remembered that she was a good student; she had won the citizenship award last year. I asked the question anyway.

"Everything OK at school?"

She brightened. "There's a special two-week program for arts and literature at the university this summer, and I've been chosen to attend."

A moment of brightness. Then her eyes dropped again. Silence returned.

"Have you had any fever?"

She shook her head.

My examination showed that all was normal. I was inclined to agree with her about the virus and said so.

"You—uh, don't think you ought to do any tests or anything?"

I had answered no before the impact of what she was saying, coupled with the panic in her face, registered.

"If it's just a virus, you'll be as good as new in a couple of days. Sometimes a stomachache can be caused by lots of things, however, so just to be sure why don't you come back Friday and we'll check again and do some tests if necessary."

My response helped, at least to the extent that she could smile as she wished me goodbye.

Her growing up had caught me off guard. I simply was unprepared to think of Ellie as other than a quiet, studious, pretty little girl who sat politely with her mother and shed no tears when the shots came. Now, suddenly, she was a young woman, and I wasn't sure that I had recognized the change clearly enough to understand what she needed. As I returned her chart to the rack, I wondered if she too had the same difficulty.

I thought of her family. They all seemed alike. Her older brother was an honor student and, like his parents, was reserved and seldom spoke. All the members of the family were courteous but never spontaneous, as if all they did was calculated and planned well in advance. It was as if they did not want to make any mistakes. I wondered.

As Ellie had known, and I had suspected only as an afterthought, the pregnancy test was positive. Now she sat in my office, pale, externally calm, still alone.

"How long have you known, Ellie?" I asked.

"About three weeks, I guess. I met Tim at a birthday party. He's older than most of my friends and he would write me notes and leave flowers in my book at school. When he touched me, everything inside me cried out. No one in my family touches or holds or hugs or kisses anybody. It's unbecoming to show emotion, Mother says, but I can't help being human. I needed somebody to hold and touch me. Well, I guess you can figure out the rest."

There were no excuses in her explanation, just a factual account of what she judged to be her need for warmth and closeness. Typically, she had been unable to consider the consequences of such closeness until it was too late. The quiet, sober, unemotional girl had collided with the fierceness of adolescence, and she had no protection for her vulnerability. Her parents had encouraged a form of self-reliance in Ellie, but she lacked the ability to exchange attitudes and feelings necessary to give her self-reliance substance. Now she sat before me, forced into an independence she did not desire, faced with decisions that seemed destined to further isolate her and increase her loneliness.

The epidemic of teenage pregnancy, with its awesome consequences, is almost beyond rational understanding, so enormous is its scope. Its causes are numerous. They include broken families, little or no education about the normal functionings of the human body and its reproductive abilities, peer pressure, seductive and stimulating entertainment, the use of illicit drugs and alcohol, and an enormous self-centeredness among teenagers that craves immediate satisfaction.

But Ellie was, to me at least, not a statistic. She was the reality of that epidemic in my very presence, and I realized how inadequate my resources for her were. I had been lulled into thinking of her as a child, full of the safety of youth; I had been lulled into failing to confront the fact that she was growing up by the very propriety of her actions.

Is it possible, I wondered, that we miss the opportunity to be straight and strong with our children in those questioning and learning years just before the beginning of adolescence? Do we say "Don't do this" too much when we should be preparing them, bit by bit, for the rare beauty and wonder that comes at that age? Do we dread adolescence, worry about its dangers, view it as an evil chasm that has to be crossed, blindfolded, on hands and knees?

Is that what had happened to Ellie and her family? In their desire to avoid mistakes had they denied the fact that she would reach adolescence, with its turbulence and changes? Perhaps. I did not know. I suspect, however, that strange as it may seem, all of us, parents and children alike, awkwardly attempt to postpone acknowledging that adolescence has begun because of our ambivalent feelings about its very existence. Inevitably, in the midst of its whirlwind, we are confronted by the very things we hoped our denial would enable us to avoid.

That is what I saw as I looked at Ellie.

"Have you said anything to your mother?"

"No." She shifted restlessly in her seat, then stood up and walked to the window. Outside, it had begun to rain, and the drops trickled down the glass in long and wandering lines. Deep in thought, Ellie began tracing the patterns on the glass with her fingers, stopping only when there were too many to follow.

"I'm scared. I wish I wasn't this old."

How old? Fifteen. A child who is no longer young.

"I can't raise a baby. I can't live at home, and even if I got married, I still wouldn't know what to do. Getting married wouldn't make me any older or smarter, or help me get a job. I can't have a baby."

She had said what I dreaded to hear.

"Tim gave me two hundred dollars and I have some money I saved from babysitting. I want to get an abortion. Tim said he had heard about a woman who does them cheap but I know about a girl last year who did that and she almost died. She ended up in the hospital and now she can't ever have a baby, even if she wants to. So I told Tim I'd ask you to tell me who to call, what doctor to see. You will help me, won't you?"

There is, in the Bible, in the second book of Samuel, a rather strange and troubling story. It involves a woman named Rizpah, a concubine of King Saul, whose sons were taken from her and hanged in what was apparently some form of sacrifice to appease God and relieve the land of drought and famine. The story must have taken place during a time when humankind was struggling to believe in a God it could not see, while being confronted with a world all too visible.

I felt some kinship with that dilemma as Ellie posed her question. I do not believe in abortion; neither do I understand or accept human sacrifice for appeasement. All that has led me to become a practitioner of the art of healing, the teachings of my conscience and the mandates of my creed, demand of me that this be an incontestable belief. Now Ellie was asking me to make a decision that did not easily lend itself to the predetermined rules by which I hoped to live. I felt what must have been Rizpah's agony as she grieved for the loss of her children: Why my sons, Lord; why me?

That was the question which formed inside my mind, and which I knew had no answer other than my resolve to make the best possible choice. Such questions are always being asked and there are many who seem able to find answers in the respectability of their infallible laws and steadfast commitment to those laws no matter what the situation. I longed to join their ranks and feel that clean purity and know, always, what was right.

Ellie would not grant me that option.

Why Ellie, Lord; why me?

Using the telephone on my desk, she called to make arrangements. The clinic would see her, she said, the next morning.

"Ellie," I said finally, "about your parents. You have made some hard decisions. Will you please make another? Speak to your mom and dad and ask them to come here. We all need to talk."

True to her nature, Ellie did not answer my plea without considerable thought.

"If you think it will be of any help to anyone. Personally, I doubt it." She made no attempt to hide the bitterness in her voice.

A little over a week later the three of them came to my office. The reserve to which I was accustomed had turned to stone, and anger edged their statements.

"I have talked with my attorney." Ellie's father spoke in precise, clipped words. "My wife and I feel you had no right to shield Ellie from us. She has committed a great sin, and everyone must pay the price."

So, Rizpah, I thought, your sons must be hanged yet one more time.

It was, mildly stated, a painful session. Ellie's mother and father did not see their daughter as my patient who deserved and needed my protection and support. They paid my fee; therefore the rights to Ellie's life, at least as far as I was concerned, belonged to them. They would pursue whatever legal channels of reprisal were open to them, and they demanded that the medical records for Ellie and her brother be immediately transferred to a doctor "who would respect parents' authority over their children."

That, at the bottom, was it. Authority. A great and awesome responsibility, and I told them so.

"I hear something of what you are trying to tell me. I strongly believe in parents' being responsible people who command respect and operate with authority. That authority, however, does not come from controlling others but from the strength of self-knowledge and self-acceptance and the willingness to risk not always being right. Ellie has made a big mistake, but at least she's gotten your attention. Do you intend to go on punishing each other for what you think is 'right,' or do you have the courage and strength to break down some of those walls you're hiding behind and admit that what you truly want from each other is some simple love and affection? Try it. Who knows, you may be surprised that it won't wrinkle your best suit after all."

Admittedly, I returned the anger they had flung at me. I simply had seen Ellie hurt too much to ignore the opportunity to challenge their stance. From it, at the least, I hoped Ellie would see that committing a mistake, or "sin," did not drop her into a deep dark hole from which there was no hope of rescue.

Having seen such little evidence of emotion in this family in the past, I expected none now. I had begun to suggest that they see their minister or a counselor to discuss their concerns further when I was interrupted by Ellie's father.

Men grieve in various ways. Fortunately, for almost all of them, it has become acceptable to cry. And that is what Ellie's father proceeded to do. Great painful sobs, accompanied by drought-relieving tears, shook his body, and he made no attempt to hide his need or his relief from those whose love he coveted.

Today, Rizpah, your cry has been heard.

I left them there to start the long process of becoming acquainted with each other and to find what it would take to learn to forgive.

Ellie went back to school and did make it to the summer program for special youngsters. I saw her only infrequently after that, but shortly after graduation from high school she came to see me for a physical examination for her application to airline flight attendants' school. We talked about the day she had come to the office with a "stomachache" and the painful decisions and growth that had resulted for all of us.

"I haven't changed my mind about abortion, Ellie, and I hope that neither you nor anyone else I know is ever faced with that crisis again. I have changed in one way, however, and you are responsible. I'm not going to be so reluctant to see adolescence come or so slow to prepare for its arrival. It's a great time of life, and I'm learning to celebrate its opportunities, not fear its consequences."

Ellie gave me a brief hug and a small package, and then she was gone. Later, in the quietness of the completed day, I unwrapped her offering. On a small piece of parchment, enclosed in a frame she had made, were these words:

> I am not afraid of tomorrow
> For I have seen yesterday
> And I love today.

13

Harder Than Most

Cra-a-ck!

Hurtling over the hedge, the baseball came to rest just inches from my feet.

Crash!

Through the bushes, face flushed, uniform streaked with dirt, came the right fielder, barely halting in time to keep from knocking me, the baseball, and himself into the street.

"Sorry, sir!"

Grabbing the ball, he threw it with a savage directness that must have carried it most of the way back to home plate.

"Hey, Doc! It's me, Junior. How ya doing? Great game! I'm playin' real good. You like baseball? Got to go! Comin', coach, comin' in a hurry! Yeah!"

"Junior, get the lead out!"

This last was undoubtedly from the coach. Judging from the gaping hole in the shrubbery next to the ball field, Junior was already far ahead of his coach's commands. Judging from the cheers of his teammates, the blind throw must have been guided by radar.

Cautiously approaching the hedge, I peered through the gap to see Junior and his team march jubilantly off the field, the last player on the opposing team cut off by Junior's heroic throw. Gingerly, I retreated from the hedge and steered myself onto the sidewalk. I wondered if my choice of detours for a quick lunch-hour

walk had been judicious. Remembering Junior, however, I decided that it was indeed a good decision.
Thinking about him brought a smile, and I recalled the
first time his mother brought him to see me.

"He, uh, is not really a junior," she explained. "I
don't remember how we started to use it as a nick-
name, but he prefers it over his given one. I suppose,
since he is adopted, that it gives him an extra bit of
attachment at times."

Perhaps, I thought, but as active and bouncy as Junior was, I saw little evidence of his attending to anything or anyone long enough to attach.

"The school asked us to speak with you about him,"
his mother continued. "He is very eager to learn; he's
the first to want to try new things, and he works very
hard to please. Yet he doesn't really seem to remember things well. He bounces off the walls with his attempts, and try as he will, he just can't sit still. They
sent these reports for you to see."

Psychological profile, achievement tests, motor
skills inventory—yes, it was all there. A child on paper. Plenty of information, but of such little help.

"Do you remember, Junior," I asked, "when it was
your special time to be adopted?"

Pausing in his headlong search of the room, he
looked at his mother and laughed.

"Nah. Too young. I was a baby, wasn't I, Mommy?"

"Yes." She nodded to him in friendly, kind
acknowledgment.

Although I had attempted to secure most objects in
the room before he came, things were in a shambles
by the time Junior's visit was complete. Yet I now felt
comfortable that I understood his unique nature. I simultaneously breathed a sigh of relief and gratitude
as I became aware of the treasure made available to
Junior in the person of his adoptive mother. If ever
there was a parent able to cope with a truly hyperac-
tive child, she, with her calm strength, directness,
and spontaneous delight, was it.

"Are you aware of the test scores?" I asked her.

"Yes. Not very flattering, are they?"

I could not keep from laughing. "That's one way of putting it. Gives us all quite a challenge."

She agreed.

Junior, curious, asked about my examination and what it meant.

"Junior," I said, "you have a quick body. It is very well balanced, and you are able to run and play games and do all kinds of things that most of your friends will want to try. Like your body, your brain wants to do things very quickly, but often it gets in such a hurry that it can't remember what it just did or is supposed to do next. That makes it harder for you to remember what the teacher is trying to tell you in school, and sometimes gets you into trouble at home because you don't finish what you started to do."

"Like Jamie Wilson's snake!" Junior said. "I put that critter on a hot rock one day and he didn't know which way to go first!"

"Well, you're like the snake in some ways. Remember, you're a lot smarter than the snake, though."

Junior, however, had already lost interest and wandered into the hall, and his mother hurried to retrieve him.

I elected to treat Junior with medicines that greatly reduced his impulsiveness. Fortunately, he continued to be passionately curious, a trait, I suspected, fostered by his mother. As a result, he was promoted from grade to grade in spite of questionable scores on competency tests and the need for extra tutoring, especially in math. Sports, however, became his real outlet and source of achievement.

"Hi, Doc! How you doin'? Passed everything. Going to the beach next week. Lettered in baseball and football. How's my blood pressure? Sure is good to see you again!"

"Junior," I scolded, "slow down. Your brain is working faster than my ears can listen."

"Sure thing, Doc. Mom and Dad said I might get a car one day if I learned to drive safely. You think I could?"

Now a lean, muscular, well-built fifteen-year-old, Junior still needed to busy himself, at least verbally, as I proceeded with his physical examination.

"Want to go to college. Probably State. Yep, State sounds fine. What do you think, Doc?"

"College is always a good idea, Junior." I hesitated. "However, not everyone needs to go, you know. Sometimes the things we need to learn to make us happy are found in other places. Do you have any other plans?"

"Nope. College. That's where I belong. 'Course, you know, I have to work harder than most to learn enough to get there."

He became unusually quiet. I waited for him to continue. He possessed such boundless energy, such a beguiling and effervescent spirit, that I was unfamiliar with this more thoughtful side of his personality.

"I'm good at sports. You told me that a long time ago. I know I'm pretty hyper, too, and I try hard every day to make that energy do for me what other parts of my brain don't seem to want to do. It's not easy."

He paused, a frown on his face.

"But," he said, brightening again, "that's why I have to try harder. Okay, Doc. Thanks for the tip!"

And he was off again, energy beyond my capacity to fathom fueling his very real desire to "be somebody," thanking me for an idea that was all his own.

Such were the memories of my contacts with Junior that crowded to mind that day by the field, brought together by the baseball challenging my space on the sidewalk.

"Say, Doc, you got a minute?"

I had not noticed the baseball coach until he spoke, and, for the second time that hour, I jumped as though I were Jamie Wilson's snake on the hot rock.

"Yes, coach. Nice game. Looks like Junior's doing a fine job."

"That's what I wanted to talk with you about." The coach heaved his considerable girth through the unfortunate hedge and, sweating and out of breath, joined me on the sidewalk.

"He told you about wanting to go to college?" The question was almost an incredulous statement.

"Yes," I replied. "He mentioned something about State University. Are you thinking about a baseball scholarship?"

He looked at me with uncomprehending eyes.

"Doc, he's a great ballplayer, but you know about his tests, don't you?"

I nodded. "That doesn't seem to bother him. His mother told me that his classwork is satisfactory; he just has to work a lot harder than the rest to finish it. His drive and energy seem to be combining to make that happen. Keep me posted on the scholarship!"

Shaking his head, the coach retreated through the tattered shrubs, convinced that Junior and I were somehow two of a kind.

A little later I faced a busy day at my office.

"Before you begin," Maggie said, indicating the closed doors with full chart racks, "please call Mr. Hennings at Merryhill School. He wants to talk to you about an activity program for their older boys."

Bill Hennings was the principal of a school for special students, most of whom were mentally handicapped. What he wanted was someone to work with groups of older children to teach them physical activities and encourage their desire to participate with each other in achieving a common goal.

"Junior," I said aloud, "you have just been volunteered."

I told Mr. Hennings about Junior.

"Sounds perfect to me," he said. "Shall I call him?"

And so he did, marking in the process one more milestone in Junior's steady if slightly delayed journey to college.

Merryhill had never participated in any athletic

event, although as a certified school in the district it was eligible to do so. Thus, not much attention was paid to its appearance against Wagner High in the opening game of football season. This was unfortunate. True football fans were robbed of the opportunity to see eleven youngsters who hardly knew how to button their shirts daringly defend their goal time and again and then brazenly push their nimble, skilled opponents' line to wrest a victory and make a point. I was one of the lucky few there, and I could easily overhear their volunteer coach proudly explain the victory to an unbelieving newspaper reporter. "We didn't know as much as they did," Junior told him, "so we just had to try harder."

He was at the supermarket, bagging groceries, when I saw him a few days before the fall school term was to begin. "You gonna coach at Merryhill this year?" I asked.

"They have a real coach now. Uniforms, too. Boy, were they proud of themselves. I'll still help out some, but, as you can see, I have a part-time job. Have to pay for my gas!" He dangled his car keys for me to see. "Driver's ed teacher was really good to me. He was patient, didn't yell like some of them, and told me to take several deep breaths each time before I drove. He also told me"—here Junior smiled—"not to drive like I play baseball."

"Junior, you are needed in the back," the voice boomed over the store loudspeaker.

Like the small whirlwind he was, Junior disappeared in a flurry of movement, leaving me shaking my head and wondering. Turning with my bag of groceries, I nearly collided with a somewhat larger whirlwind in the form of the baseball coach.

"Well, you have done it now!" He fairly shouted. "Yes sir. Just look at this. Do you have any idea what this is?"

"Coach, please stop waving that letter in my face. Of course I don't know what it is. I don't have X-ray vision, you know." Exasperated, I leaned my bag of groceries against a lamppost and waited.

"You put him up to coaching those retarded kids, didn't you? Well, it's true, isn't it?"

"I don't think 'put him up to it' is the right phrase, but, yes, I suggested him for the job. Why are you so upset about it?"

"This letter," he said, shaking it in front of my nose to emphasize each carefully enunciated syllable, "is from State University's athletic department. They want me to allow Junior to play in an exhibition game to try out for a scholarship. They say," he fairly hissed, "that he is known as an all-around, complete athlete."

"You worried about that, Coach? Sounds like a real feather in your cap to me."

"You know what I mean. He won't pass the competency tests this year, and then where will Junior and all your tomfool ideas be? Me, I'd rather not get him all excited and then dash his hopes for all the world to see."

He sighed, shrugged his shoulders, and departed.

Admittedly, the coach had a point. Neither of us was interested in seeing Junior placed in a position from which retreat would appear to be disgrace. However, I trusted the judgment of the young man enough to feel that he would, in spite of his charging impulsiveness, weigh carefully the opportunity he was offered before he acted. As it turned out, the coach really felt the same. In spite of his blustering manner, he ached for opportunities for his students, and Junior, on the ball field at least, was one of his best. He described the offer to Junior matter-of-factly, then set about doing his best to get the boy ready.

I was out of town and did not hear the results of the game or Junior's performance in it until a week later. His mother broke the news in a conference with me.

"I know you like baseball and I'm truly sorry you

missed seeing them play." She had been waiting patiently to tell her story. "Junior was superb." She beamed with delight as she continued. "He threw out two runners all the way from right field and hit a single and a double! The coach at State as good as promised him a scholarship. Now comes the hard part." Her excitement ebbed a little. "You will need to write a statement in support of his application. What—what will you say?"

"The truth," I answered easily. "He is a gifted and exceptionally talented young man who has a remarkable amount of insight into what works for him and what doesn't. That kind of truth will keep him focused and continue to channel his abundance of restlessness into productive results. Junior is unique. State University is fortunate that he wants to accept their invitation." I thought for a moment before adding, "He always seems to get that extra bit he needs from somewhere, and I don't expect that to change."

She stood, thanked me for my help, and turned to leave. I knew she had always dreaded having the diagnosis part of his physical examination forms completed, and the one for the college admission was no exception. My words had visibly reassured her. She paused with her hand on the doorknob and spoke.

"It's hard for all of us to understand that being mentally retarded does not automatically mean being a failure at life. For Junior, I think it has simply been a challenge. He never assumes he is handicapped."

"I know. For Junior, being mildly retarded has meant only one thing."

"Yes." She laughed, her good humor restored. "For him, it has simply meant that he always had to try just a little harder."

14

Emergency

Two A.M. Please, not now. Just a few more minutes. Please.

The persistently ringing telephone ignored my plea. Likewise the wide-awake secretary on the night shift at the emergency room. "Hold for the nurse, please," she told me. The nurse came on the line.

"We have an eight-month-old baby. Cute little thing. Fever of one hundred and four, and she's very fussy. The parents are new in town. You're on ER call tonight. Sorry."

One of the hardest things about getting out of bed in the middle of the night is getting out of bed in the middle of the night. Grumbling, I nearly tripped on the dog, illegally sleeping at the top of the stairs. Fortunately, the cold night air cleared some of the sleep from my brain and allowed me time to marvel at the beauty of silver moonlight searching for the tunnels beneath the towering oak trees that line my street. Partly appeased, I sighed and headed toward one more confrontation with fever.

"Her name is Megan. She started throwing up this evening and then felt real hot. She's about to burn up with fever."

"Uh-huh." I nodded.

Burning up with fever. Hard to believe that such a frightening symptom is most often the body's way of killing the invader threatening its existence. With twinges of sleep still blurring my grasp on reality, I thought idly that the human race owes much of its survival to the ability to respond to infection by "burning up with fever."

The young parents holding their tired and irritable daughter were obviously in no need of a philosophical discussion about humankind's methods of avoiding disaster, no matter how much it applied to their present situation, especially one initiated by a stranger they were called on to trust at two in the morning.

"Has she had her baby shots?" I asked the routine question. The answer, like the question, used to be a routine yes. Now, however, a generation of protected youngsters have grown to parenthood without personally doing battle with whooping cough or diphtheria. They know no fear of these insidious and malevolent forces; instead, they develop first a suspicion and then an angry mistrust of the very agents that have protected them. Routine immunizations are no longer, it appears, just routine.

Almost against my will, I closed my eyes and remembered.

"For God's sake, hurry!"

Terrified, I felt the tread of feet and heard the splash of steaming water poured into a basin. Hair streaming from steam and dripping sweat, my mother held the nearly lifeless form of the son just older than me in the vapor. Blowing in his face her own life's air, she coaxed and willed him to live. His purple lips and thin heaving chest sucked at the oxygen she offered, holding on with a will that only those not mortal understood. I do not remember how many nights they struggled as my skin crawled with fear. I only knew that diphtheria was a word filled with dread. When an immunization against it became available, my generation wept with relief that our children would not face its torturing grip.

Routine immunizations? Hardly.

"Yes, she's had her shots. What do you think is wrong with her?"

"Not," I muttered to myself, "diphtheria. Or whooping cough, or polio."

I finished my examination of the baby. Fussy, but alert. I even managed to encourage a smile by making some funny noises, so things did not look too ominous. A blood count and urinalysis added to that reassurance, and after a bottle of cool juice she drifted off to sleep. Before the clock's hands had reached three, the relieved parents had departed with an appointment to see me the next day if they needed to check in. I turned toward the sliding doors, which snapped to attention to allow me passage.

Still, I lingered for just a moment. I could not help but contrast my presence in this modern and sophisticated place of healing with the memory of a kettle of steaming water and the vigil my mother had kept.

"Out of the way! God help us! Somebody do something, please! Oh please, dear Jesus, don't let my baby die!"

Knocked against the wall by the burly body rushing through the doors, I hesitated, then turned to evaluate what was happening. He was big and bearded and soaking wet. Tentatively and as unobtrusively as possible, the pretty girl with him offered to the nurse an equally wet and struggling bundle securely wrapped in a blanket. Sputtering, the child tried to get free, wailing, "Mommy, Mommy."

"She didn't lock the gate to the swimming pool. I've warned her, but she is disobedient. Joshua walks in his sleep and he fell into the pool. If he's drowned, I'll kill her!"

Joshua was certainly not drowned. His lungs sounded quite clear, but I decided a chest X-ray was needed to make sure no water had been aspirated into his lungs.

"No!" thundered the voice behind the beard. "X-

rays are known to contain evil spirits. The devil will
not enter my son through your devious ways!"

Believe it or not, his name was Samuel. I knew that
before getting a full dose of religion, he had been
known to do more anointing with a full bottle of beer
than with anything similar to the methods of his ancient namesake. At this hour, however, I had no pa-
tience with either of his choices.

"Stop it, Sam! Joshua is not drowning, as you can
very well see. I need the X-ray to make sure he hasn't
sucked any water into his lungs. Anyway, the only evil
spirit I see around here is your obstinance, so behave
yourself!"

Chastened, Sam agreed to the X-ray. As I had
hoped, the film was clear.

"No harm done, it seems. Now I want to know what
this is all about, and why, Sam, you come screaming in
here threatening to kill Elaine. What in blazes is happening to cause all this commotion at three o'clock in
the morning?"

"Well, I was really scared, Doc, I admit it. I know
I'm big and strong and not supposed to be afraid of
anything, but when I saw Joshua fall in the pool, I lost
it. We couldn't sleep, Elaine and I, and we were sit-
ting by the pool arguing. I guess Josh heard us and got
out of bed to see what we were doing. The gate wasn't
latched. He tripped on a hose, and in he went."

"Doesn't sound like Elaine's fault to me. Are you all
having marriage problems? Is that why you were up
so late?" They nodded. Elaine said nothing. Eyes
tired, shoulders slumped, she hardly seemed to care.
Sam continued to talk, trying to justify himself by
once again reverting to his prophetic stance.

"She won't stay home. She says she has a right to
work. The Bible says wives should obey their husbands, but she says she's a grown woman and won't be
treated like a child."

"That's right," Elaine said suddenly. "I swear, Sam,
you're an idiot. Can't you see I'll be a better mother for

Joshua if I'm happy about what my life means? It's important for me to be able to do things for others."

I interrupted their exchange. "Sam, it seems to me you've gone from one extreme to the other. I'm very pleased to know that you have a sense of belonging and a cause to defend, now that you are a religious man. One word of caution. It's easy to forget that other people can be motivated by a response to God equally as powerful as yours, but on an entirely different time schedule. So don't try to make others over in your image, assuming it's God's word you are speaking. I'm not a minister, Sam, but if I had one sermon to preach, that would be my theme. Joshua needs both of you, and he needs you as a team. I really believe that Elaine is not nearly as interested in a job as she is in having you respect her as a person with strengths and judgment, an equal. A person to share life and its happenings, not someone to continually struggle with and do battle with, trying to decide who's in command. I think, if memory serves me correctly, the same fellow who talked about women being submissive to their husbands also said that God was no respector of persons; that is, God showed no partiality to anyone. Think about that, Sam. No one has the upper hand when it comes to modeling our lives after that kind of leader."

I hadn't meant to preach, but obviously I had. Sam seemed doubtful. Elaine merely tightened her hold on Joshua. I did notice, however, that after paying their bill, they headed toward the parking deck side by side and hand in hand, Joshua sleeping soundly on his father's shoulder.

"How long do you think that will last?" Chin propped in her hands and elbows braced against the reception desk, the head nurse stared after the departing couple.

"You have any idea?" I answered.

She shrugged. "Well, obviously I don't care much for the attitude that says women should stay home

and just be servants. Yet I do sense in him a desire to
be an authentic man, not just a male provider. Does
that sound irrational?"

"I don't think so. Go on."

"He's strong and big. And scared. What he would
like is for God to wave a magic wand and clear up the
concerns he has about how he is supposed to act, his
confusion about the image he projects, and especially
the doubts he feels about trying to be a husband and a
father. His strength lies in seeking, his weakness in
wanting the answers now. Do you think"—she suddenly sat up straight—"that he would actually harm
Elaine?"

"Possibly. He's very impulsive. Elaine's pretty sen-
sible, though. I rather think she could talk Sam into
not doing something he'd regret."

"Do you know them well?" she asked.

"So-so. I remember when they were married. I
read about it in the paper. Their families are quite
well known."

"Hmm. Do you think they will stick with their new
church?"

"I suspect that is what has given Sam the urge you
saw stirring in him to be accountable for his actions,
so I hope so. I truly wish for him an opportunity to
struggle with the meaning of his feelings, in company
with people who can help smooth off some of those
rough edges we have just seen. I'd be quite discouraged if his search led him to nothing but the forming
of rules and the spouting of laws."

"Speaking of laws," she replied, "I think someone
has just broken their quota for tonight."

I followed her gaze to the doors, again open wide,
through which rushed a blur of people surrounding a
careening stretcher on wheels. The crimson stains on
the white sheets spread as we watched, spurring the
attendants to haste. I retreated and left the new arrival to the precision and skill of others already effi-
ciently in action.

"Just kids. Prowling around in the wee small hours when they should have been home in bed. Ran through a stop sign and crashed into a tractor-trailer rig. No seat belts. Their only protection was just the Godawful notion that being young they'll live forever. And then I have to come along and pick up the pieces! I'm sick of it, you know, mister? Sick of picking up the pieces. Isn't there any sense left in anybody?"

The state trooper, his young face already hardened by experience, stared at me for a moment. Expecting no answer and waiting for none, he turned, reports in hand, to follow the action. I watched until he disappeared. This time I passed unhindered through the busy doors and made my way to the doctor's parking deck. Tiny fingers of gray seeped through the black sky, and from somewhere a blue jay looking for an early meal warned of the passing of night. Three A.M. was long gone, and a part of me had already begun to dread the weariness I would feel when the clock's hands reached that number in the afternoon. Another part of me, the part that felt like a breathing, living echo of myself, held to the drama of life seen at times when the facade is transparent and the makeup missing. A time would come, I knew, when the weariness would win. But for now, life at three in the morning had a clarity that gave me a reason for doing battle with the other hours of the day, focusing the mind and heart to the courage necessary to pick up, once more, somebody else's pieces.

15

When Commitment Becomes Real

Searching my pockets, I found a few pieces of loose change and hurriedly dropped them into the plastic bucket. The bell ringer, nose and cheeks alive from the chill in the air, breathed a frosty "God bless— merry Christmas!" as I pushed into the mall. People everywhere, rushing like ants, slowed my progress, but I finally reached my objective.

The small card and gift shop near the southern end of the mall was less congested than the teeming passageways but still enough swollen with last-minute shoppers to make moving about difficult. Sighing and regretting that I had joined the Christmas Eve Club once again, I set about trying to find what I thought I wanted.

"'Scuse me, sir. Ain't you the fellow that doctored my kids a while back?"

The voice came from a tall, thin man with watery eyes and a scraggly beard of several days' growth. His attempt to smile revealed the slight tremor of his lips, and several of his teeth were on their way out. His coat, although worn, seemed sturdy enough for the unusually cold weather we were enduring. Searching my mind, I tried to place him.

"Oh, yes," I said finally. "The Department of Social Services. I remember. We met with you and your children, and I gave them their checkups before school. How—uh, how is everything?"

"Well, sir," he replied, "I'd be lying if I said things was just fine, but they could be a whole lot worse. Me and the kids is together, and they're making it in school, and I've had work most every day."

He seemed interested in telling me more and, in spite of the hour and frantic stream pushing past, I found myself wanting to hear it. I had had only the one contact with him, and no word about the children after their physicals had been completed. That had been in the middle of a hot and irritable week in August when he had appeared before the child advocacy team to petition for the return of his children. He had just been released from the alcohol detoxification program of the local mental health unit, and I remembered that his face had the same rough growth of beard then that I now observed.

"Wasn't much to look at, was I?" He grinned; his response was surprisingly shy and youthful. "I admit I was plenty scared. Alice—she just flat walked out.

" 'Them kids is yours, you take 'em.' That's all she said. I didn't even have a place to sleep, so the welfare office put the children in foster care."

A quick glance toward the coffee shop next door revealed two empty stools. I motioned quickly and he followed, shifting the packages he carried to a more comfortable position. When we were seated, coffee steaming in front us, I urged him to continue.

"I guess," he said quietly, head lowered a bit, "a lot of us fellows just get going on the wrong foot and don't much think about how to stop it. It's always easy to find someone to take a drink with, and you always figure the woman will stay home and take care of the kids. When Alice left, I nearly ran too; probably would have if I hadn't just been let out of the detox center. Then I looked at them children—Mark, Sue, and Lenny—and I realized I was their daddy and didn't any more know them than if they was strangers. The way they looked at me, they must have felt the same. They didn't cry or carry on or nothing.

They just stared at me, waiting. When they left for the foster home they didn't even look back."

His fingers were curled tightly around the thick white mug; he seemed lost in the memory of his awakening to a responsibility he had no idea existed.

"It was the idea that they didn't expect anything from me at all that did it. If my own flesh and blood didn't care what I did, what did it matter to anyone else?"

There was pain in the question and I sensed he was still asking it, while trying, ever so slowly, to make it disappear.

"So I set about seeing if I could make a go of trying to stay sober, get a job, and make some kind of home where they would feel cared for."

The refrain of Christmas carols drifted through the open doors of the shop, carols sung by a high school chorus clustered around a traditional manger scene. The music made me remember. He was right. I and others on the team had been very skeptical of his ability to provide stability for his three youngsters—or to even remain on the wagon, for that matter. We had thought they would be better cared for in a foster home. "No crib for a bed," the singers chorused, and I thought how nearly I had kept him from finding any room, either for himself or his children.

"Plenty times I wanted to quit. The oldest, that's Lenny, he balked at everything I'd tell him. Seemed to dare me to make him mind. Said he hated me, wished I was dead." He looked me squarely in the face. "Any of your kids ever said that to you?"

I shook my head.

"Hope they never do," he said, and the defeat he had felt crept into his voice.

"What did you do? Did anyone help you? How is Lenny acting now?" I felt impatient to get the answers, aware that the crowds were beginning to thin slightly as Christmas Eve drew on.

"I didn't know what to do, so I took him fishing. Just

me and him. I know how to fish and camp, so I figured to do what I was good at. First night it rained and stormed real bad—lightning and thunder and a lot of wind. He was plenty scared, and in spite of himself he held me real tight. After that night he seemed to feel better about things. I think he realized that if I could protect him in a thunderstorm, he could trust me to do the same in other places."

I urged him to continue. "And the others? What about them?"

He drew a small, neatly wrapped package from the bag.

"It's a teddy bear." Gently he shook the box, and I could hear bells jingling faintly.

"For Susie. She lost her old one. Softy was his name. She carried him everywhere, tucked under her arm; it was kind of a way of inviting people to notice her, I guess. She'd talk to him, and then she'd pretend he was telling others what she said. I always thought that was her way of feeling safe and still holding on to people she needed. When Softy turned up missing she didn't cry or act like she'd lost a thing. She just stopped talking. At first I wanted to shake the words out of her, to make her say something. You see, I need them kids to talk to me too."

He sat staring into his cup, remembering, the ragged edges of his hair sticking out from beneath his cap.

"What I did was hold her, tucked under my arm like she was Softy. I talked a lot, nonsense mostly, trying to remember what I felt like when my dad came home drunk. Bad, afraid, not wanting to talk. Lonely for a hug or a kind word. Remembering about that made me want to forget it, and it was all I could do to keep from drowning myself in another bottle. Somehow I held on. I guess I knew she needed me, and I was beginning to know how much I cared about her. Finally she started to say a few words. 'Me and you and Softy is going to have a picnic. You fix samitches, and I'll bake a pie.'

"She'd say stuff like that, and I thought the young'un was losing her mind. I tell you, it was scary. But at least she was talking. And Doc, I ain't had much school, but I'm not dumb. I could tell she was trying to say real important things to me in the only way she knew how. So I'd hold her and rock her, and she would talk. Finally it all came bubbling out, the way she was scared about no one wanting her, no one taking care of her."

"You want anything else?" The waitress, cleaning cloth in hand, tried to be polite but I could sense that she was eager to finish up, to leave the shop and do whatever she needed to bring a touch of specialness to the part of Christmas Eve she owned.

"Thanks, we're finishing. Merry Christmas," I said. She smiled in response, then left the ticket and moved to the far end of the counter, wiping as she went.

"Well, she still gets scared at night, and she's going to need this teddy bear clear into grade school, but she ain't lost her mind."

I knew triumph, especially in the eyes of one not used to winning. So, I thought, there is a strength in you that we, the others and I, did not see. I was aware that his children were challenging him to grow even stronger. I also sensed that his response to that challenge was driving him away from the oblivion of alcohol and toward encounters with life and that life for the first time promised excitement and offered meaning to tiring days and lonely nights. I waited for more.

"Mark seemed to make friends with me the easiest. I think the foster home he was in those few weeks was good for him. Or maybe it's just the kind of person he is, 'cause he seems to make friends wherever he goes. Anyhow, I have a job doing tree work. I ain't afraid of heights so it's an opportunity for me. In the winter I cut and sell firewood, and Mark goes with me to deliver it. He sure is a good salesman. He'll go right up to somebody's door and just stand there, looking up with his big brown eyes. I swear, I believe I'd buy stuff from him myself when he does that."

Was he thinking that he could have been that kind of boy, one people naturally warmed to, if given a chance? Was the pride he felt in the youngest of his children helping him build his own self-esteem?

"Guess what I got him for Christmas." He grinned through his ragged mustache. "A pickup truck. He loves my old truck so I got him a toy one just like it." His smile faded and his features softened. "Lenny was hard for me to think of what to get. Then suddenly I knew what would be a way of telling him I understood about things." He pointed to the rod and reel poking out from the top of the packages.

I nodded. "I think Lenny will understand," I said.

"Thank you." He looked me straight in the eye, and I knew he was thanking me for more than the coffee. "Maybe we'll see you again sometimes." He picked up his packages and turned to go.

"You know this street?" I scribbled my address on a scrap of paper.

He figured he did.

"I'm fresh out of firewood. How about a load for me? Uh, for a fair price, of course."

He laughed a rich, joyful laugh.

"Sure thing. Guess we *will* see you again. First of the week OK? All right, then. Merry Christmas!"

The crowd swallowed him. I only had time to see the square set of his shoulders and the purposeful march of his feet, my "merry Christmas" lost in the ringing of bells, the blaring of piped-in holiday music, and the noise of busy people, before he disappeared from view.

I returned to the card shop. Only a few minutes remained for shoppers to make their last hurried purchases. Now, however, I would not be rushed. Neither Christmas nor my visit with the man bearing gifts for his children would tolerate hurry. I could buy things another day. Time to be with my family suddenly seemed all-important. Turning toward the door, I headed back into the crowd. If someone hadn't banged into me at that moment, causing me to look down, I would have missed the tiny counter display at the very front of the shop. Miniature wooden figures knelt on cotton snow, partially encircling the fragile cradle. A fold-out card served as a backdrop of sky and stars. Across the top of the card were the words of the shop's familiar slogan, "When you care enough——." The man with the scraggly beard and bad teeth had lived those words, and his children had become a bridge to sanity and a new life. That seemed to be a fair assessment of the season, and I left it at that. Satisfied, I too moved with squared shoulders and purposeful steps to Christmas and to home.

16

Beth Is Her Name

Folding chairs were placed neatly in front of the platform, but most of the observers chose to lounge on blankets covering the thick green carpet of grass. Children were twirling, leaping, and turning cartwheels, trying to match the rhythm of the sounds coming from the strange instrument played by the man in the colorful pleated skirt. Soon their attention and that of the crowd was drawn to the piper. He and several others began to play in concert—a tune of anticipation and proud admiration. At just the right moment, the lithe figure of a girl, auburn hair streaming in the breeze and Scots plaid brilliant in the sun, stepped forward, bowed, and took her place on the stage.

"Ladies and gentlemen, boys and girls," shouted the first piper, "Here to dance to the tunes of her ancestors is the very talented young Beth!"

The applause was enthusiastic, and for good reason. Beth was indeed talented and every graceful movement of her flying feet, moving to the ancient music of the pipes, brought forth cries of pleasure.

No one could have been more pleased than her parents and I, as we watched the leaps and twirls, the toss of her hair, the graceful movement of her head and neck. And as we watched, we remembered the night she was born.

"She's breech. First baby. No choice now; labor isn't happening."

Mask hanging loosely beneath his chin, the obstetrician spoke matter-of-factly.

"Ready?"

I nodded, secured my own mask, and followed him into the operating room.

Seconds became minutes as the quiet, efficient activity proceeded around me. Instruments passed from the careful hand of the scrub nurse to the busy one of the surgeon, and soon the baby was among us. Her cry was muffled by the warm blanket held by the nurse from the newborn nursery, and I relaxed, knowing that the baby did not need my help to start breathing.

Her name was Elizabeth—for her grandmother, they had said—"but we'll call her Beth."

A quick look reassured me that her breathing was normal, and with a finger held to her tiny chest I felt the surge of her heart. No one commented about the peculiar tilt of her head or the crazy angle of her legs. She was, after all, breech, and that had been expected.

X-rays confirmed what I had detected, only it was worse than I thought. Both hips were completely dislocated, and the cups of bone into which the femurs were supposed to fit were distorted and inadequately formed. In addition, the lower left side of her face was pushed inward, converging on the twisting, tightening edge of the muscle shaping her neck.

"Breech. Dislocated hips, and torticollis to boot. Not much meat on your bones either, Beth. And I've already been told about your keeping half the babies in the nursery awake last night. I believe your mom and dad had a tiny bit different picture in mind of how you would be, so there's work to do with you. Now keep quiet and let me do the talking."

She made no sound as I carried her to the formal introductions, perhaps because she was very securely wrapped in two layers of blankets. Whatever the reason, and it was a fortunate one, she continued to be quiet, allowing her parents to get a sense of perspective which, as it turned out, would be sorely needed.

"Beth," I said reassuringly, "this is Mom and Dad. Folks, this is Beth."

She squirmed a little, blinked at the light from the windows, and waited. Each in turn held the child, rolling her name around in their hearts so it began to obscure their vision of the cockeyed head and awkwardly protruding legs.

"Beth." Her mother breathed the name softly and, exhausted, lay back against the pillows. Dad, Beth, and I worked our way back to the nursery.

"I'm having an orthopedic specialist consult with me in the morning. Her hips aren't resting in their sockets properly, and we need advice about the best choice of treatment. Dislocated hip problems are often seen in babies who come into the world upside down. You noticed that one side of her neck is shortened and the head pulled to that side? That is called torticollis. I'll begin showing you how to manage it as soon as you both feel up to it."

I spoke as if we were discussing the weather. They needed to understand the problems their child faced in architectural terms, definable, understandable. That, I hoped, would relieve some of their anxiousness about her gawky appearance.

"She—uh, she's not crippled or anything, is she? I mean, she will be able to walk and all, won't she?"

We sat down outside the nursery, able to glance through the viewing windows at a variety of infants, all hungry, assembled in line, ready to be taken to their mothers. He watched them intently, trying in vain to find one who looked like Beth.

"Yes. She'll walk. No, she is not crippled. I understand your concern and want you to answer that same question for Beth's mother. Somehow I think she would prefer that reassurance from you right now."

He agreed, with a sigh. Tired eyes and a stubble of beard told me he'd had a long night too.

"I'm going home to bed. Will the orthopedic doctor be in before I get back?"

"Probably late this afternoon." I waved him toward the elevators and turned to reenter the scrub station between the two nurseries. Through the glass door I could see Beth, face red and furious, hands tightly clinched, shaking the bassinet with her squawls.

"She's a handful, doctor. I hope it means she has spunk and spirit, not just the irritables. Glad it's them and not me. Eight hours a day is enough. I'm too old to carry on all night like this."

Gently Mrs. Nelson cradled Beth in her large sturdy arms, and the infant quieted.

"Like a kitten, you are, child. Pick you up and all I hear is a purr. Put you down and it's the squawls again." She eased herself into one of the numerous rocking chairs and began rocking back and forth, back and forth, until the rhythm claimed Beth and she slept.

"Your telephone isn't going to get much rest from this one," was Mrs. Nelson's parting remark as I headed for the elevators.

Her prediction proved correct. The first phone call came the same day Beth and her mother were discharged.

"She's spitting her milk. Are you sure that's OK—I mean with her neck twisted and all?"

Reassurance. We had talked about all that and more, especially the casts which kept the legs firmly positioned like a frog ready to leap.

"That keeps the head of the femur, the thigh bone, in the right place for the molding of the hip portion of the pelvis," I had explained. "If all goes well, that will permit a proper union and the hips will be firm and strong. Now let me show you again how to put just the right pressure on the jaw to stretch this stubborn neck muscle."

That had been the easy part. The real difficulty had been predicted by Mrs. Nelson. Beth's constant irritability and demands for attention, made worse by her inability to relieve her frustration by kicking, quickly eroded her parents' reserves of good humor. Something else must be wrong with their daughter, they decided, and I just wasn't telling them what it was.

"You're not trying to protect us from something, are you?" There was an edge of annoyance in Beth's father's voice.

"I don't need to protect you from anything. You're tired, disgruntled, uneasy, and probably afraid too, but you're not in need of protection. Are you concerned about the colic?"

They nodded. Beth had begun to time her outbursts so that they coincided perfectly with the end of the day's work for Dad and the preparing of the evening meal by her mother. The result, they said, was a lot of cold dinners.

"Do you remember the poet Longfellow?" I asked. "He wrote a poem called 'The Children's Hour.' In it he described the joyful, peaceful end of the day, with blissful children surrounding their doting parents. Either Longfellow didn't know many children or he was never home for dinner at his house. What you're describing is not unusual. Many other families have experienced the same thing. In fact, one family I know calls it the gangrene hour!"

Finally, Beth's parents laughed. It was probably the wrong thing to do, however, because Beth was startled, and the session ended with the shrieking, wailing, red-faced frustration that made them and every other parent of a "colicky" child fear disaster.

"Just a few more weeks," I called after them, "and Longfellow's version will begin."

Colic is a word borrowed from the ancient Greeks. Loosely translated, it means intestinal pain, which may be why the abdomen and its contents are blamed for the symptoms. I have a notion, however, that the irritability and fussing, accompanied by the legs being drawn up to the stomach and every muscle straining until the baby explodes into red-faced crying, which seems to build to a climax at day's end, is more a sign of stimulation and response than of stomach pain. Like their adult counterparts, babies have different responses to their surroundings and different ways of expressing them. They haven't had much experience in deciding which responses are appropriate, and some babies are such go-getters they let loose with everything their nervous system can produce. Somewhere in the neighborhood of three to four months of age, however, the symptoms disappear. I suspect that comes about because the brain has developed further, and because the baby is establishing more trust in those who are providing care. With Beth, then, and others like her, I could speak with reasonable assurance that the "gangrene hour" wouldn't be around forever. My notion seems confirmed, too, by the fact that a rocking chair and a soothing voice seem to do as well or better than all the formula changes and drugs so frequently prescribed.

Beth took longer than most, but when the time came for her six-month checkup, her parents reported that evening meals were no longer a dreaded part of the day's activities. She had replaced crying with babbling and seemed to concentrate as much energy as possible in her eyes, fixing everyone who came close with an intense and curious gaze.

"I feel so helpless," her mother commented. "About her hips and legs, I mean. I just know she aches to kick and roll over, and what will happen when she wants to crawl? We're to see Dr. Lesley this afternoon, but I know he isn't anywhere near ready to talk about getting rid of these casts."

She pointed to the rigid plaster molds, braced to keep Beth's legs at the proper angle, that definitely prevented any movement that would resemble a crawl.

"And what about walking?" Beth's mother was almost in tears. "She'll never learn to walk or run or jump or play hopscotch. Isn't there anything we can do to help her get well faster?"

Firmly but gently, I reminded her of Beth's course of treatment. "From the beginning we've known that this would take time. And, quite honestly, we aren't out of the woods yet. Sure, she'll walk, and run too, but there is always the possibility of some difficulty persisting, and she may have some awkwardness to deal with. Because we've known about her problem from the beginning of her life, rather than discovering it when she was six months or a year old, she does have a head start and a better chance of being normal. Incidentally," I said, changing the subject, "I notice you're doing a very fine job with the neck problem."

As if in response, Beth turned toward my voice, fixed a piercing gaze on my face, and then broke into a big smile. As she smiled, I saw that her face was more symmetrical, fuller, and beginning for the first time to reveal the beauty to come.

"Thanks. I don't mean to complain, and I know we are fortunate that her problems are no worse than they are. It's just that—well, you know, everybody expects their baby to be perfect."

"I'll call Dr. Lesley tonight," I promised, as we were saying goodbye. "I'm eager to know how much progress she's made in getting those new hip sockets formed too."

But it was not nearly enough.

"I'm sorry," Jim said. "I just went over the X-rays again with the radiologist, and we're making too little progress. I called my old chief at the center where I trained. He's something of an authority on this problem, and I've made an appointment for Beth and her family to see him next week. He thinks surgery may be necessary to shape the contours and provide a snugger fit."

The surgery went well, but Beth had not been happy with the IV tubes and had jerked them out three times before a venous catheter had been securely fixed. Even less well did she like her new casts, which seemed even more rigid than the others. She showed no signs of discouragement, however, and as the weeks passed she became very adept with her hands and arms. Shut off from one area of expression, she eagerly searched for and found another. This was probably, I thought, one reason she had been so fussy earlier. She obviously possessed a mind that was always searching and responding, and that may have been why she was so easily stimulated to react. Whatever the case, she maintained a steady outpouring of activity, reaching, throwing, sorting, and conquering an ever-increasing variety of toys and games. No one would have disputed her claim, if she had desired to voice it, of being national pegboard and push-the-shapes-through-the-funny-hole champion!

The return visit to the medical center produced cautious optimism. The new CAT scan revealed good socket growth. Only a few worrisome areas in the bone formation were noted. About these, Jim would only say, "We'll see."

"We'll see" turned into a second round of surgery, and this time Beth ran out of steam. She retreated. Quiet, merely pushing at her food, eyes large and hurt, she simply waited. She made no attempts to pull out the IV tubing and managed only a hint of a smile when Donald Duck came to visit. Her parents, alternating shifts at her bedside, called me.

"She just wants to be left alone. The orthopedic surgeon says he thinks the problem is solved now, but if Beth doesn't care, what difference does it make?"

At first, no thoughts came to me. I tried to reassure them, to suggest a special toy or a visit from a friend, but no idea of substance seemed to form. They thanked me anyway and hung up, but not before I heard the fear in their voices.

The next morning pushed along slowly. Near its end I watched a toddler, mother in tow, waddle down the hall.

"Doesn't he walk beautifully?" She watched in obvious admiration as the little fellow, with his brand-new ability, took one step too fast and plopped onto the carpet. "He just started yesterday," she said protectively. "Come on, Robbie, show the doctor how you can really walk!"

Whether Robbie was interested in showing me anything was immaterial; what did interest him was the encouragement in his mother's voice, and that gave me an idea. As soon as they left I was on the phone.

"Do you remember," I said, "when you first met your daughter? As scrawny and upside-down as she looked, you accepted her as Beth, as the person whose potential you had dreamed about encouraging, as someone you actually knew. I think Beth needs to be reminded of that now. Tell her her name, over and over again, and what you see in its richness and the pride you have in it. She needs to remember who she is."

Three days later they were home from the hospital. More furiously than ever, they reported, Beth tackled puzzles, took apart toys, and used large crayons, keeping busy the hands that drew her attention away from her legs, immobilized in their new plaster. "Beth do it, Beth do it," she'd say, and indeed she did.

That surgery was the last. Finally, her legs were released from their white prisons and therapy begun, to strengthen their flabby muscles and steady their wobbly gait. Time after time she would fall, and bruises covered her knobby knees. She would become furious at her weakness and hurl her toys at the walls in anger. She screamed at the physical therapist, but always came back with a hug or two. She kicked in the whirlpool until water sloshed over the sides, and she refused to be carried, crawling when no handrails were available. She knew that she was Beth, and that Beth, as she continued to say, would "do it."

The dance that sunny afternoon came to its end. Amid vigorous applause, Beth came to greet us. Her cheeks were flushed with pleasure, and her clear blue eyes only accented the rich auburn of her hair. The tartan of her ancestral clan, rich with colors, did not compete with the health and vigor of her own resplendent youth. She accepted our compliments with enthusiasm, said she had friends to meet, and thanked us for coming. Then she turned to her mother and laughed. "That dance," she said, "is a big hop, skip, and jump from what we once thought, isn't it?" And with a swirl of plaid, she left to join her friends.

17

Investing in the Future

"Child can't rightly hep it, Doc. She has them seejurs and wets herself and then gits sent home. Makes hor fccl plum foollsh, the other kids laughin' and all. Teacher been good to us, but she says they is a limit."

I nodded, understanding that he was telling me several things at once. "What about the medicine?" Her seizures hadn't seemed especially difficult to control, and I was surprised that such little progress had been made.

"Well, you see, honey, it's this way."

I groaned to myself. Every time old man A.C. came in there was a new brand of trouble, and when he threw "honey" into the conversation I knew the dark clouds were thickening.

"Brenda Jane," he continued, "that's Effie's baby, she took sick with a fever and we rushed her to the 'mergency room. You remember Effie? She took up with that Marine and followed him clear to the coast. He warn't no good, I guess, 'cause she came back and had Brenda Jane and he don't even write her, 'cept at Christmas."

I waited. Experience had taught me that trying to rush A.C. would only extend the visit. Besides, I had grown to admire the old fellow in spite of the haphazard way he lived and managed the half-dozen or so grandchildren who called him "Papa." Once, at his

invitation, I had paid him a visit. The house, venti-
lated by gaping cracks in the weathered siding, sat at
the end of a dusty, rutted road. Two old cars, neither
with wheels, flanked the doorway, while a rusty
pickup truck, sagging on worn-out springs, sat by the
edge of the road. It apparently provided the only
form of transportation. More dogs than I had ever
seen in one place lay in the shade of the house, and I
remember three or four of the youngest children
fighting over who got to ride next in a worn-out tire
that hung precariously from a poplar tree. Disorder
prevailed, and that seemed to suit them just fine. Except in the garden. There I stepped into another
world.

"Nice, ain't it," he said. It was a statement, not a
question.

"It certainly is." I wandered down well-spaced
rows of corn, between huge hills of cucumbers, beds
of lettuce, patches of strawberries, and tented poles
overrun with beans. In spite of the heat, the plants
were well watered and lush.

"How do you manage to do so well? I mean, who
helps?"

You'd be surprised how much water them kids can
haul from that old springhouse." He pointed toward
a small hump in the ground on which a tarpaper-
covered frame was built. "That and my social security
check keeps us off the welfare."

I remember how he had looked then, with his white
hair stirring in the wind, his weather-beaten and
wrinkled skin, his gaunt but erect frame, and his faded
army jacket draped over his shoulders, and felt rather
proud to know him. Even if he did talk forever.

"Brenda Jane, well, she had the pneumonia. Had to
have penicillin shots, and they allowed as how I had to
pay cash. Cucumbers ain't in yet, and social security
check won't come till next week, so couldn't buy no
more of them blamed pills to stop them seejurs."

His defiance protected his pride. I knew there was

little point in suggesting that he call the social services agency. I had offered that advice once and he
had quickly squelched the idea. Pointing his finger at
my face, he had roared, "You think I'm a no-good ig-
nernt? Them youngsters is in this world on accounta
me and they is my responsibility!" He had empha-
sized the last word with a proud squaring of his
shoulders. So this time I simply asked if he had any
ideas.

"Well." He settled back into the softness of my office chair and rubbed his chin slyly. "As a matter of
fact, I do. Futures."

"Futures? What futures? I'm sorry, I don't understand what you mean."

"Cucumber futures. You know, like them pork
belly futures I've heard about on the television. I
sell you shares now, and when the cukes are ready,
why, you come pick all you want. Same with anybody
else you want in on the deal. You've seen my garden,
and you know I ain't cheatin' nobody. Better deal
than that torn-down stock market anyhow. This way
nobody loses."

Fortunately, Maggie popped her head in to say I
was needed elsewhere, and I escaped before laughter
overwhelmed me and made A.C.'s offer appear foolish. Actually, I reasoned later that day, the plan did
have merit. So I signed up for his futures market, hoping as I did so that the price of cucumbers would not
take a nosedive and that the enterprise would buy
enough medicine to ward off the "seejurs," at least
until next season's crop.

A.C. and his concerns soon drifted into the back-
ground. All I later recalled of that spring was the unusually dry weather and pesky cover of clouds that
seemed intent on dulling the dogwood's bloom and
keeping winter clothes in fashion. The rest was lost in
days of coughs, fevers, and the early onset of an outbreak of spotted fever.

"I really hate to bother you at dinnertime, but we

just got Janie from the day-care center and she doesn't look at all well. What should we do?"

Janie's family had been camping a week earlier. When they returned, a wood tick came with them, firmly attached to Janie's scalp. The incubation for Rocky Mountain spotted fever was well within the time between discovery of the tick and their phone call. I judged it best to meet them at the hospital right away.

Indeed, Janie did not look well. She frowned from the pain in her head, and tensed her aching, inflamed muscles. Her skin was flushed and bore, around the wrists and ankles, a faint suggestion of purple dots. Her eyes, staring through half-closed lids, had a reddish tinge and lacked their usual brightness.

"Janie, can you hear me?" The evening shift nurse, white uniform covered by a colorful smock, leaned close to the child. Janie mumbled but was simply too tired to open her eyes.

"We're going to give you a tiny shot in the arm, and it will hurt a little. I don't want you to be surprised."

Deftly, she inserted the needle, drew off several small tubes of blood, then connected the syringe to the clear plastic end of the IV tubing. Ampules of antibiotics were injected into the bottle of fluid, and the steady drip, drip began. Tiny molecules moved to wage chemical warfare against the unwanted invader while Janie slept and her parents kept a vigil.

Before leaving, I spoke to the nurse. "How long have you worked the evening shift?"

"About a year," she answered. "I don't have any children yet, and this time of day gives me a chance to pretend I'm a mother sometimes, getting the children to sleep, reading them bedtime stories. I'm sure I get conned into that a lot, but I don't mind."

"I'm grateful to you for talking to Janie the way you did. Sometimes people hear when we think they won't; it's important that a sick child know when something is going to happen. They already have enough to cope with without becoming afraid of those who are helping to make them well."

She nodded in agreement and moved off down the hall toward the light of another room, carrying, just in case, a copy of *Bedtime Stories for Children.*

Janie's recovery coincided with the return of early summer weather: some showers and, finally, blue skies. Various and sundry viruses, along with their friends the spotted fever germs, took a holiday, and a welcome break gave the office staff a chance to go home early. Maggie was just locking up when the answering service called on the private line.

"Well, OK. I'll give him the message. Thanks for the call."

"What's up?" I asked, noting her concerned expression.

"It's A.C. He's at the VA hospital. Admitted this morning with chest pain. Does he have a history of heart problems?"

"Not that I know of. I'll go by the VA and see him. As I remember, it's down by the river. Ought to be a pleasant drive on a day like this."

A.C. was wired to several monitors, each of which raised an alarm every time he raised his voice, which was often. I finally told him that it was either me or the buzzers, so he quieted a bit, though he still grumbled about his predicament.

"Ain't no heart attack. Tried to tell them doctors it was my indigestion. You see how much attention they paid to me? Why ain't you out with the rest of them quacks, playing golf?"

Only one thing could make A.C. that abrasive. He was worried, and he was trying to hide it.

"Easy now, A.C. What's really getting to you? Why are you in such a frenzy to be gone?"

Even before he opened his mouth to speak, I knew the answer. Cucumbers!

"It's the garden, Doc, and them futures. Who's going to see to it? This has been the dryest spring I can remember, and we was having to haul water from the creek, cause the spring was getting awful low. Doc, this ain't no way to be. I got to get back there and hep. Them young'uns can't do it by theirselves. Can't you do something?"

He lay back, his leathery face closer to the color of the pillow than the hue imparted by the outdoors he loved so well. He picked despondently at a fragment on his bedcover, and sighed. "I guess I'm a little tireder than I thought. I 'preciate the visit, Doc."

The EKG and enzyme studies failed to verify A.C.'s diagnosis of indigestion. He would be needing a lot of recuperation, which did not include hauling buckets of water to his thirsting plants. That presented a challenge to his family, especially the young'uns. I thought I would try to reassure him by telling him his customers would, in all likelihood, be happy to wait until next season. He would have none of that, however, and reverted back to his "I did it; I'm responsible" attitude. I didn't push, so it rested at that, and I wondered just what would happen.

A few days later I received a short letter from A.C., scribbled on a piece of paper torn from a sheet of hospital doctor's notes.

"Deer Doc, how are yu?" it read. "They aim to let me out next week. If you ain't busy (ha!) I'd be obliged for a ride home."

There was no ignoring that challenge. A.C. was dutifully bundled into my car on the appointed day, and we headed out. He was unusually quiet, a fact I attributed to his illness and the sobering prospect of going home to a new way of life. With A.C., however, such observations were usually mistaken, so I ventured no comments as we drove.

The dogs were the first to greet him, followed quickly by the grandchildren and a host of their friends, who ranged in age from those in diapers to nonchalant teenagers. He seemed to know all their names, and numerous rounds of hugs and handslappings took place before he could find a seat. This turned out to be a well-cushioned rocking chair strapped to the frame of a wagon of sorts. He hardly had time to settle into it before he was whisked away toward his garden and the real surprise of the day.

Tied to the gatepost with rusty wire was a pole with a banner, hand-lettered, that read, THE FUTURES BE-LONG TO YOU. WELCOME HOME PAPA!

They pulled the wagon up and down between the rows, pointing to various spots where growth was particularly abundant, answering his questions and telling him over and over again how they had enlisted help to haul the water and keep the garden protected.

"We bargained, Papa, just like you. We got chicken futures, milk and butter futures, and any-stuff-out-of-this-garden-you-can-name futures. Why, when we started lettin' the word out that ole Judy would be available to coon hunt, even them lazy Wallaces hauled water for two days. We sure done good, didn't we, Papa?"

Unable to trust his voice, A.C. nodded his head vigorously up and down. Satisfied, the youngsters began to scatter, only to remember the wagon and then finally to return it and its cargo to the house. They watched as their grandfather ambled onto the porch. The excitement of being home and the substantial greeting of his grandchildren had lifted A.C.'s spirits, but now he was ready for a rest. For a little while, though, he sat in his favorite cane-bottomed rocker.

"Doc, honey, do you allow I did it on account of jus' the money?"

I didn't answer his question for quite a while. We rocked slowly, watched the sun set, and listened to the night sounds tune up for their concert. He had needed money for medicine, that was true, and I had thought the cucumber futures a rather cunning way to get it. I had underestimated his wisdom, however, and had misunderstood the opportunity he had provided for those he claimed as his responsibility. Of course, he hadn't planned the heart attack, and he had been afraid it would derail his carefully manufactured scheme. Now he and I saw just how effective his planning had been and how well his goal had been met.

"If you mean, do I understand that you are trying to teach them about being responsible, yes, A.C., I see it. From the looks of things around here, I'd say they rather enjoyed the lesson, wouldn't you?"

I didn't go to the farm again. In early summer for several years after that, however, a bushel or so of cucumbers, large, green, and shiny, found their way to my door. I never inquired about paying for them. When you invest in futures, the dividends, it seems, just keep on coming. Which, of course, was exactly the way A.C. intended it to be.

18

June Bug

"He your dog?"

"Yeah. Ain't much good, though. We keep him 'cause we need a watchdog."

It was hard not to laugh. The boy's statement, spoken in seriousness, was hardly appropriate. The dog, an emaciated, flop-eared black mongrel, tail tucked between his legs and eyes constantly on the defense, seemed more in need of protection than capable of providing it.

"Does he have a name?"

"Uh-huh. We call him June Bug, 'cause he ugly like a bug and we got him in June."

"Well, OK. Nice seeing you." I jogged on, completed my lap, and headed home to shower, breakfast, and work.

June bugs. Oh, yes. I remembered june bugs.

"Shh. Don't move. See, there it is!"

Sweat rolled into my eyes, dry, raspy leaves of corn sawed at my hands and neck, and powdery wild daisy pollen threatened to force a sneeze that would violate the command to be silent.

Stealthily, my brother reached for the shiny green beetle and expertly captured it before it could fly to safety. A thread retrieved from the bib pocket of his faded overalls was quickly tied to one leg of the struggling creature. Holding the end of the thread, he released the bug. Into the air it went, only to be forced to dip and circle and amuse us with its struggles to be free, until either we tired of the game or the june bug lost its leg.

Hot summer days on the farm were not, I remembered, without some adventures, and june bugs contributed their share. They were probably not as exciting as a mongrel watchdog on a rope, but they were important enough to be one of my childhood's happy memories.

Perhaps because I had spoken to him, he waited at the same spot, the little black dog still attached to a ragged piece of rope. Perhaps I had hoped he would appear, hence the small dog biscuit tucked into the pocket of my jogging suit.

He waited for me to stop, not wanting to seem too obvious.

"Esther said I shouldn't talk to strangers. You ain't one, are you?"

I smiled. "No, we're friends now, I guess. How is June Bug?"

"Ah, he ain't no good. Big kids throw rocks at him and he just hollers and runs under the house. Esther said we ought to take him to the pound."

"What do you think?" I asked the question gravely.

"Everybody needs a chance. Maybe he'll learn."

"Who is Esther?"

"Stepmother. Her and Paw took up together last year and got married. She got a girl. Name's Ida. That ain't no Bible name, is it?"

"Don't think so." I reached into my pocket and offered June Bug the biscuit. His tail unwound enough to waggle a few beats of "thank you" as he gulped the treat.

"Sorry, June Bug, I only have one. More next time."

"I knew it. She tried to act smart and say her name came out of the Bible. Wait till I see her."

"How old is she?" I asked.

" 'Bout ten, I guess. She tries to boss me all the time."

"Well, good luck." The two of them stood, unmoving, as I jogged off.

He looked to me to be about nine or ten himself. Except for his eagerness to talk and his very obvious interest in June Bug, he would have escaped my notice. His clothes weren't very colorful, his hair was a muddy brown, and his face seemed so ordinary as to defy description. I wondered then if the rocks being thrown by older boys were directed only toward June Bug.

I tucked two biscuits away for June Bug next time, and their appearance was greeted with a great deal of frantic activity on the part of the previously subdued tail.

"Ida's mad. She says you must have read the wrong Bible." I detected a spark of animation in the lackluster eyes. He must have won a small victory for a change, I thought. Come to think of it, June Bug seemed to have changed a bit as well.

"What's happened to June Bug?" I asked.

"Oh, I gave him a bath. He don't scratch so much now."

I bent down to pat the dog's nose. He responded with a friendly lick of my hand.

"School's gonna start soon. Wish summer would last forever." He wiggled his bare toes in the grass next to the path that ran through the park where I jogged.

"You like school?"

"Not much. Don't do too good. Last teacher I had, 'fore we moved here, yelled a lot. When I couldn't figure out my homework she'd spank me for being lazy. Paw was gone to work a lot and couldn't help me, and Esther—well, she don't do too good at reading either. I just as soon stay home and be with June Bug."

"Where are you going to school?"

He told me and I made a mental note to call the principal, a friend, and have her keep an eye out for the boy.

"I think you'll like that school. I know some teachers there, and one of them has a dog that looks a little like yours. Maybe she could be your friend too."

He did not seem impressed, but he was unwilling to drop the conversation; as I started off again, he and the dog followed.

"Why you run so much?"

"It's good for my health. Besides," I said, smiling, "I make some really neat friends."

The boy and Ida had declared a truce and June Bug was up to three biscuits and looking less like a waif by the time school started. I had called the principal, but, interestingly enough, she already knew the family.

"He's not a good student," she had told me. "Troublemaker, too. Put firecrackers in the boy's bathroom, put a frog in the teacher's purse, and supposedly stole lunch money from his classmates. He was suspended for being absent too often. What? Oh, sure, I agree." She had laughed. "Sending someone home because they've been staying home doesn't make sense to me either."

"I can't judge his ability to learn," I told her, "but the boy is no troublemaker. Look at June Bug and you'll know that."

"Who," she had asked, "is June Bug?"

But before I could reply, other more pressing demands claimed her attention, and a stack of health certificates for kindergarten students claimed mine.

"Can you imagine," Maggie asked, pointing to the forms, "what it would be like to shepherd thirty of those wiggling little creatures five full days a week? You complain about being awakened at all hours of the night, but I'd like to see how patiently you'd put up with them during the day!"

"Maggie, you have a talent for getting to the heart of every matter. I grant you that teachers play very important roles in the lives of children. Sometimes I think we are too complacent in understanding the significance of their position or the demands placed on

their abilities. Often they are the ones who first rec-
ognize when things aren't going well in the life of a
child and his or her family, and their response to
whatever need they observe in the child is indeed
crucial to the outcome of the situation. In the same
way, teachers are in a position to excite minds to learn
and to encourage attitudes of respect and acceptance
of others, just as they accept and respect the great variety in the children they teach each year. Some
teachers," I continued, "like some doctors or lawyers
or whoever, fail to understand how truly awesome in
the eyes and minds of children they are. Did you
know, Maggie, that I taught school one year? No, not
kindergarten, but a classful five days a week just the
same. The first teachers' meeting was an example of
what I mean about not understanding. The principal
summed up his instructions to us by saying, 'It's a long
time until next May, and I warn you, it's the teachers
against the students.' "

"You made that up," she said.

"No. It's the literal truth."

"I see. Like some doctors I know who are short on
bedside manner, is that what you mean?"

"Exactly."

"That places a great deal of responsibility on teachers for things other than just seeing that Johnny learns
to read, doesn't it? By the way, what kind of teacher
were you?"

"Rather good, I think. They gave me a party at the
end of the year." My excitement in remembering the
event caused her to laugh.

"Why?" she asked. "Was it because they were
sorry to see you leave or happy that you were not
coming back?"

As day came calling the next day, vapors like the
ghosts of night rose quietly from the lake, and a few
ducks stretched their necks and nudged each other
into activity. I shook the stiffness from my legs much
earlier than usual and ambled instead of jogged into

the park. The ducks scattered noisily at my approach, bringing a scowl from an equally early fisherman. I had not expected June Bug and the boy, even on such a fine Saturday morning, and was rather surprised to see them waiting in their usual place. Nevertheless, I had a few biscuits in my pocket, and June Bug ran happily to meet me. His coat shone brightly, and he sported a new collar.

"Hey, June Bug. Where did you get the new collar?"

"Did the principal call you?" the boy asked anxiously, not even taking time for a greeting.

"No. Was she supposed to?" I asked.

"It's about June Bug. He wouldn't stay home when I went to school. Every day he would stay at the door of the school, or sometimes he would sneak into the secretary's office and go to sleep under her desk. He ain't had no shots or nothing, so they took up a collection, and my class took him to the vet. That's where we got his new collar. Principal said, since June Bug was part your responsibility, she 'spected you to help pay on him too. That's why I wanted to warn you."

"Thanks for telling me. How do you like your new teacher?"

For the first time since I had met the youngster, his face lost its anonymity, and he broke into a smile that rivaled the brightness of rays of the early morning sun bouncing off the surface of the lake.

"You know what she told me? She said I was a great reader, and just needed more practice! Here, look!"

I had not noticed the book beside him. As he reached for it, I began to realize that this was the real reason he was waiting so early and so eagerly. He had an accomplishment to share, one he had begun to fear would never be.

I listened.

"There was a big house. A boy and a girl lived there. They had a dog." He stopped and grinned. "Like Ida and me, and June Bug too! 'Cept our house ain't very big."

"So what do you think?" I asked him.

"Looks like school may be a good idea this time. My teacher tries hard to help all of us. Kind of funny thing she does. She don't yell or holler or carry on and everybody is a whole lot quieter. Ain't nobody gettin' paddled in her room neither!"

He spoke with admiration and conviction.

"Does she have any dogs now?" I asked.

"Yep. Two. Roscoe and Isabelle. They ain't mutts, though, 'cause she got papers and all on them. They're show dogs. She said 'spose to be a festival in this park right here next month and she gonna show her dogs then. You coming?"

I nodded. "What about June Bug? I think there's a category for dogs who don't have papers. Why don't you enter him?"

"Can't. Cost five dollars and I ain't got it."

Using a scrap of paper, I wrote a telephone number for him. "Lady needs help cleaning her garage. You look strong enough to do the job. She'll pay at least five dollars."

"Thanks." He and June Bug were off like clouds before a strong wind.

Come on, legs, I thought aloud. You won't get any younger by envying them their speed.

A knock on the door interrupted two-year-old Kimberly's exam and I turned to screen the interruption.

"I'm sorry," Maggie said, "urgent phone call." She pointed to the one closest, in the lab.

"This is Larson in the ER. I've got a boy here with a dog that has been hit by a car. The boy is fine but the dog needs a vet in a hurry. Boy won't budge until he sees you. He keeps jabbering something about a june bug."

"I'm on my way." Turning to the nurse, I said, "Maggie, please explain what's happened to Kimberly's mother and finish Kimberly's lab work. I'll try to be back soon."

An ambulance screeched by the corner and pre-

ceded me up the ramp to the emergency room en-
trance. Vaguely, I noted that the afternoon shift was
changing as I pushed my way through the doors. I
found June Bug, the boy, and a girl I suspected was
Ida, waiting in Room Five.

"What happened? How is he?"

Wordlessly, they drew back the towel covering the
small burden they carried between them. June Bug's
eyes, filled with pain, flickered in recognition, and his
tail tried desperately to greet me. No use. He was too
far gone to do anything except whimper.

"Ain't nothing to be done, is there?" The boy's
voice had a defeated sound that seemed to say one
ought not to expect too much, or losing would just be
too hard to accept.

"No. I'm sorry. But he's with his friends, and that
makes things easier for him, don't you think?"

They both nodded. After a while, we wrapped the
dog in a towel and I walked them to the door.

"I'm going to take him to school," the boy said,
"and we'll bury him there."

A few days later, the principal called to ask me to
stop by the school for a visit. She wanted to talk about
the boy and all that had happened.

"I was afraid he would shut down," she said. "The
dog seemed to help him focus and make him feel both
wanted and needed. His teacher encouraged his feelings about his pet as a way of stimulating him to learn
and be involved with the other students. He truly
seemed to respond, and, like you thought, exhibited
none of the behaviors we'd been worried about. So
when the dog was killed, I expected some aggression
and even went so far as to suggest to his teacher that
she be especially cautious with him."

"What did she say?" I inquired.

"She laughed. Actually laughed. 'Did you watch
the burial?' she asked me." My friend continued.
"Seems it became a project for the entire class. Several of the children brought pictures of their pets to

share, and others carried rocks and placed them to make a permanent marker for June Bug. Afterward they had a picnic lunch, brought by some of the parents. The class has continued to talk about June Bug. Other children who have lost pets, and even some who have lost family members, have learned to speak more openly about how it feels to lose someone or something important. That boy is part of the group now; June Bug's death does not belong to him alone."

"Thank you for telling me," I said, as I stood in preparation for leaving. "Reading and math are important parts of school. Yet learning them seems related to the community that exists within each group of students. It appears that June Bug has been a means of developing this particular community, especially for his young master."

"That reminds me," she replied. "Would you be very surprised if I told you that one of the parents helping with the picnic was Esther?"

The park was filled with sound, color, and activity, and the festival, as always, was a great success. The teacher's dogs, Roscoe and Isabelle, must have enjoyed the spectacle more than usual, for when I stopped by the show ring, both sported award ribbons on their collars. Maybe the extra help in getting them ready and the obvious affection and encouragement provided by the boy contributed to their success.

"We won two ribbons, a red and a blue," he said proudly. "Aren't you going to give them biscuits too?"

What was it he had said about his dog, when Esther had suggested that June Bug had belonged at the pound? Oh, yes. "Everybody needs a chance. Maybe he'll learn."

"I like the way you speak now," I said. "That's also a very nice shirt." I stopped just short of telling him that his face had somehow become quite handsome as well.

"I bought it with my own money. I work every Saturday. The lady you told me to call has a lot of friends. Looks like I'll be cleaning out garages clear into next summer." He paused. "Bought something for Ida, too."

He grinned, and there was no mistaking the mischief in his eyes.

"What is it?" I asked.

"A Bible. Written in regular English. Now she won't have any excuse to make about what's a Bible name and what isn't!"

Wintertime jogging was sporadic. Crepe myrtle, florescing pink and red, bordered the lake by the time my efforts again became more consistent and predictable. Now, as I had done during the dreary days of January, I glanced ahead to the turn in the path, just in case the boy might be waiting. He had not shut down, as his principal had feared. His school record, I had learned, was satisfactory, and he had emerged as a bit of a leader among his classmates. That was plenty to keep him busy and make him feel welcome. Still, I missed the two of them, the nondescript boy and the scruffy little dog.

"What you running so fast for?"

I had not thought to look on the park bench and nearly passed them by.

"Well, hello," I said. "That your dog?"

"Yes. Just a mutt. Went by the pound last week and there he was."

"He have a name?"

"Yep. See?"

Neatly engraved on the plate attached to the little black dog's collar was JUNE BUG II.

"Thought you might want to meet him, just in case you got a lot of dog biscuits left. Well, have to go. It'll take both of us to clean that garage today."

I called after him, "You going to give him a chance too?"

"What do you think?" was his answer as he went his way, June Bug II running to keep up with his master.